MW01056911

DON'T TAKE YES FOR AN ANSWER

DON'T TAKE YES FOR AN ANSWER

USING AUTHORITY,

WARMTH, AND ENERGY TO GET

EXCEPTIONAL RESULTS

STEVE HERZ

HARPER BUSINESS

An Imprint of HarperCollins*Publishers*

DON'T TAKE YES FOR AN ANSWER. Copyright © 2020 by Steve Herz. All rights reserved. Printed in the United States of America. No part of this book may be used or reproduced in any manner whatsoever without written permission except in the case of brief quotations embodied in critical articles and reviews. For information, address HarperCollins Publishers, 195 Broadway, New York, NY 10007.

HarperCollins books may be purchased for educational, business, or sales promotional use. For information, please email the Special Markets Department at SPsales@harpercollins.com.

The names and identifying characteristics of certain individuals have been changed to protect their privacy.

FIRST EDITION

Designed by Elina Cohen

Library of Congress Cataloging-in-Publication Data has been applied for.

ISBN 978-0-06-286971-5

20 21 22 23 24 LSC 10 9 8 7 6 5 4 3 2 1

TO MY WIFE, RAQUEL—
WHO THANKFULLY TOOK YES
FOR AN ANSWER ON OUR
WEDDING DAY.

CONTENTS

There are certain people you meet in your life who just care. They care about other people, they care about humanity. They care about making the world better.

There are other people you meet who just seem to be connected and always seem to know everyone that you know. Somewhat like "six degrees of separation" or a spiderweb through relationships.

Steve Herz is one of those rare people who encompass both of these qualities. I have known Steve for more than twenty-five years as we grew up as "competitors" in the business of media representation. But he was never a true competitor. He was someone that I respected and someone who always exhibited ethical behavior.

Fast-forward to 2016, after I had left IMG after a thirty-year career. I decided to start my own company, the Montag Group, and Steve and I agreed to merge our talent businesses together. It has turned out much better than I expected and Steve has become a kindred spirit in the growth of our company. The business of client representation is far more than just deal making. It is a true service industry where to get to the very top, you have to take a sincere liking and dedication to your client to make them the best they can be at their craft and take them to levels that they only dreamed of. Steve knows how to make people better. He knows how to make people better communicators, he knows how to make people better broadcasters, he knows how to help people get more out of their careers and their lives. Steve is a true people person.

We live in an increasingly tough and difficult world on many different levels: politically, socially, and in our professional lives. Businesses have become extremely competitive and cutthroat. It is hard to get a good job and it is equally hard to maintain it.

In his book, *Don't Take Yes for an Answer,* you will hear from some of the greatest minds in the world on how they communicate, how they lead, and how they achieve the highest level of success in their personal and professional lives. Steve has the ability to draw these lessons out of these leaders and I believe that after you read this book, you will have a different outlook on life and how you can get and make the most out of each and every day.

—*Sandy Montag, CEO of the Montag Group*

DON'T TAKE YES FOR AN ANSWER

Some people come home from dinner with friends carrying a doggy bag. I tend to come home with bruised shins, reminders of my wife's well-placed kicks under the table. You know the kind. It's the universal technique a spouse or partner will use to quietly signal that it's time for you to shut your mouth and stop embarrassing them. Regretfully, my wife has had plenty of opportunities to perfect her aim, given that like curmudgeon Larry David in the TV show *Curb Your Enthusiasm*, I have a tendency to be a social assassin. A social assassin is someone who lays waste to the social niceties and white lies that frequently smooth human interactions. For example, if we're at dinner and you ask me if I like your new hairstyle, I know I'm supposed to say, "Yes, it looks great!" And I will if I really do.

But what if I think it looks like you took a weed whacker to your head?

I won't tell you that, because I'm not a mean guy.

But I am an honest guy.

So I will answer honestly that no, your new hairstyle isn't that flattering, I liked it the other way.

That's when my wife will kick me.

Hey, you *asked*!

In my defense, I spend most of my life telling people hard truths, and it can be challenging to remember that outside the office, even when I'm asked, not everyone actually wants to hear them. As a talent agent, however, it's my job to point out any elements that could hurt my clients' careers, whether it's their appearance and dress, their body language, their speech patterns, or their vocal tone, and let them know what they can do to improve so they can deliver their best performance. My company, the Montag Group, represents more than 250 of today's top journalists, broadcast executives, and media personalities—the very faces and voices you've grown to trust and rely on to keep you in the know at CBS, CNN, MSNBC, FOX News, ESPN, and elsewhere. Beyond our broadcast division, which is one of the largest in the industry, we provide guidance to athletes, technology companies, law firms, and international banks, along with top CEOs and entrepreneurs. By and large, most of my clients are already considered stars in their chosen field (though many have been with me since the beginning of their careers), but they still seek out my professional assessment and coaching methods because they believe that, despite all the applause and approval they get from peers, friends, and supporters, and despite all the success they've already enjoyed, they can still do better. That desire to do whatever it takes to excel is the difference between people who are good at what they do, and people who are great.

If you're reading this book, my guess is you want to be the latter. So here's my first piece of advice:

If you want to find out what you're truly made of and reach your utmost potential in work and in life, you must stop taking YES for an answer.

For reasons we'll explore in this book, we get a lot of positive feedback that we don't actually deserve, which means you can't trust all the yesses you hear. In fact, if you've checked off all the obvious boxes necessary for a stellar career in your field—education, credentials, years of experience—but you still aren't where you want to be, that lack of honest feedback is probably part of what's holding you back.

Because face it, if you're doing just fine but you're not truly killing it the way you always dreamed you would, I don't care what anyone else tells you, you're doing something wrong.

Don't you want to know what it is?

If you're frustrated because you're falling short of your potential—whether that means you're getting passed over for promotions, failing to close on new business, being denied pay raises, struggling to retain customers and employees, negotiating ineffectively, lacking positive professional and even personal relationships, or generally not getting the respect, acknowledgment, and recognition you desire—and you want to know why, you have to be willing not only to accept criticism, but also seek it out. You have to find someone who cares enough to tell you when you aren't all that, and accept that a "no" is often more helpful than a "yes."

I came by this knowledge the hard way. In fact, I owe my entire career to a boss who would not give me the "yes" I expected to hear.

It was August 1990, the summer after my second year at Vanderbilt Law School. I was one of twenty-nine summer associates at the law firm of Curtis, Mallet-Prevost. It was a prestigious program and my fellow wannabe lawyers and I each hoped that upon graduation we'd be offered a high-paying first-year position at the Park Avenue firm. Typically, 90 percent of the associates were offered a job. Good odds. Nevertheless, it was still a competitive environment, and as the summer program rolled to an end, naturally the lot of us became anxious as we prepared for the "last rites."

Turner Smith was managing partner of the summer associate program, and it was he who would deliver our fate. On that hot August afternoon, I was the last associate called to his office. By then, however, news had already filtered through the building that every single one of the summer associates had been given an offer. I felt confident as I took a seat in his office, ready to enjoy the moment. Smith was a disarmingly charming man, almost courtly, and he welcomed me with a warm smile. He leaned forward across his walnut brown desk to look me straight in the eye, and in a gentle, polite tone, he told me I was an atrociously bad summer associate. I should save my money and quit law school. Immediately.

Come again?

I sat back in his stately leather chair, wide-eyed and incredulous. He again smiled politely and underscored his point—I shouldn't consider, not even remotely, becoming a lawyer.

It felt like a ton of bricks had been suddenly smashed over my head. How could this be? I'd scored in the 95th percentile on the LSATs. Twenty years of formal schooling had all led in this singular direction. I came from a family of legal experts. My father, my uncle, brothers, and cousins were all lawyers! My whole life had seemed preordained to a career in law.

I reeled out of Smith's office, trying to process what had just happened. I was days away from starting my last year of law school, and the tuition was paid. I was going to get that law degree. But then what? A black mark like this on my record would be tough to explain away to any other law firm. After mulling over my options, I hit on a plan. If I couldn't be a lawyer, I'd follow my other lifelong dream. Sports had always been my first love. The overweight youngest of three boys, I'd made up for what I lacked in athletic ability with sheer passion and knowledge. In school I'd done every sports-related job you could do except play, from serving as sports editor of the yearbook and newspaper, to statistician, and I'd often fantasized about becoming a sports agent. Why not go for it? My law degree would be a marketable asset in a competitive field.

Fast-forward five years, and I was twenty-nine years old, beginning my fourth job representing sportscasters at a boutique talent agency. Each job made me more miserable than the last. I'd thought I'd learn to develop and nurture sports talent, but all the companies I worked for cared about was whether you could bring in enough clients to substantiate your salary. Beyond that, it was negotiating boilerplate contracts and glorified babysitting. Despite rubbing elbows with people whom just a few years earlier I would have killed to meet, I found the work expected of me utterly uninspiring and, worse, pointless. Stuck at home one day with a nasty head cold, I realized that I had to get out while I had little to lose, or risk a lifetime of regret. Before I could talk myself out of it, I called my boss and quit. He graciously offered me severance through the end of the year.

Once again, I found myself unmoored.

The next day, feeling better, I put on my yellow headphones, turned up my Sony Walkman radio, and jogged over to the brand-new Reebok Sports Club I had joined a few months earlier, which featured this new thing called a "Spin" class that was all the rage. On my way to the reception desk, I found myself sharing the elevator with a familiar figure. It was Alfred Geller, a widely respected agent for several top television newscasters, such as Al Roker, Connie Chung, and Maury Povich. We'd met briefly at a media conference a few months earlier. At nearly three hundred pounds, he was literally and figuratively a giant in the industry. I took his appearance as a sign.

The elevator ride was only two floors up. I had thirty seconds to make my case. I pulled off my headphones.

"Alfred," I blurted. "So nice to see you again." I told him that I'd quit my job and wanted to start a talent agency representing sportscasters. "With your knowledge of newscasters and my sports expertise, we'd be a great combination."

The elevator doors opened. Geller stepped off and turned back to look at me. "Be at my office eight a.m. tomorrow morning," he said.

For the next eight months, I studied at the altar of Geller, receiving a virtual PhD in every aspect of on-air communication. His approach to talent representation was nothing like what I'd witnessed at the other agencies. Certainly, his job entailed brokering favorable contracts—he was a beast at the negotiating table—but his core mission was to do whatever it took to make his client better. Period. His philosophy was "If you build it, they will come." He meant, build yourself up into something outstanding, irresistible, or indispensable, and the world and the marketplace is yours.

He obsessed over the details, reviewing hundreds upon hundreds of audio and video tapes with his clients, analyzing and critiquing every nuance of their delivery and on-air work, from the resonance of their voices to their posture. He demanded perfection, and he got it. Through him I met luminaries like Lilyan Wilder, Mort Cooper, and Sam Chwat, voice and speech trainers to stars from Charlie Rose to Julia Roberts. I devoured their books and took additional courses at New York University, from acting—so I could learn a little about how my clients do what they do—to voice—so I could understand diaphragmatic breathing—to meditation—so I could be sure to slow down and make careful observations (helpful for someone like me, who runs with a fast motor). I wanted to learn everything I could about the art of presentation and making powerful first impressions.

Eventually I concluded that Geller's exclusive focus on his clients' on-air performance didn't go far enough. I didn't think it was a coincidence that broadcasters who treated waiters and assistants as graciously as they treated their producers rose faster and further than those who selectively turned on their charm only if they were in the presence of someone with power. It told me there couldn't be a disconnect between who our clients were on-air and off-air. Any incongruence meant they were faking half their lives, which not only had to be exhausting, but could also create professional barriers. Our reputation does not only stem from how we behave, speak, and present ourselves when we're "on," but also from how we behave, speak, and present ourselves during the small, perhaps seemingly inconsequential interactions we engage in during our day—in the hallways, at the conference table, during the business lunch, at the networking function, and even in our interpersonal relationships. While our "on-air" performance has to make the right impression on our audience, our "off-air" performance has to make the right impression on the people who may hold our career in their hands, if not now, then someday. To really help my clients, it would not be enough to extract an excellent performance out of them; I'd need to mine them for all-around excellence.

With that philosophy in place, I left Geller and opened my own agency, which I named IF after Rudyard Kipling's poem by the same name, which says, "If you can dream—and not make dreams your master . . . yours is the Earth and everything that's in it." From day one, my aim was to provide people with the honest feedback and clear signals they needed to allow them to become the best version of themselves, so they could achieve their dreams and shift their lives from average to exceptional. This is what Turner Smith had done for me, and it felt fitting in my new role as a professional talent agent and coach to similarly honor others by dealing straight—that is, by being more helpful than nice. As IF built its client base, I became increasingly convinced that how we perform when we think no one is looking, and the impression we make on others, holds the key to career success. It was the only answer I could find to the question, What makes one smart, hardworking individual more valuable to an employer than another with a seemingly identical profile? What makes one good apple better than the rest of the bunch?

Eventually we expanded from working exclusively with sports broadcasters and media talent to other professionals in various fields because I discovered that the key to becoming a superstar manager, salesperson, or CEO is no different than the key to becoming a superstar broadcaster: you have to get your audience, of one or a million, to trust and believe in you. That means your educational proficiency and specialized skill set will only get you so far. They're the price of admission. It's your ability to reach, persuade, and influence, the way you communicate and engage with the world, the way you show you give a damn, that makes all the difference in a career that sputters and one that soars. To stand out and excel, to get the attention of those who will help you move up, protect you during lean times, or compete for your talent, you need to perfect your AWE.

A—Authority. W—Warmth. E—Energy.

Over the past two decades, AWE has become the prism through which I observe, assess, coach, and grow every single one of my clients. I listen for it when we're analyzing recordings of their voice, and I look for it while observing them perform simulated interviews, meetings, or sales calls. It takes a special person with a thick skin to work with me. I'm always respectful, but I pull no punches. Because of this, I've been hired and fired on the same day by people who were too accustomed to hearing "yes." But those professionals who have stuck with me, who have refused to take yes for an answer, have seen their stars rise. And now I want to do the same for you.

Don't Take Yes for an Answer is a self-empowerment and self-assessment guide to achieving your fullest professional and personal potential for anyone who's doing just fine but who wants to do *amazing*. I'll show you how AWE-inspiring actions, words, body language, and new habits can elevate how impressively you are seen, heard, and received. And not just when you're presenting as a keynote speaker or in a meeting, but in private—when you interact with individual clients, colleagues, and friends, and even with the casual acquaintance like your Uber driver. Drawing on my time-tested rules and advice, along with real-life examples of when you have it and when you don't, and backed by research in the fields of social science, I'll show you that the connections you make through "private speaking" are often the ones that can most significantly propel your career and personal life forward. You will learn a tried-and-true formula for success that will both incrementally and dramatically change the way you perform in all aspects of your life.

The good news is that the space between good and great can be quite narrow. Often, a small tweak, a gentle adjustment, is all it takes to upgrade the trajectory of a career. Once you build your self-AWE-wareness and learn to increase and improve your AWE—and everyone can—you become the magnet in the room, the person whose ideas are valued and taken seriously, who speaks persuasively and impactfully, the person everyone wants to be around. It just takes practice. I make this bold claim without hesitation because I've seen this methodology work on celebrities, politicians, broadcasters, CEOs, and ordinary people of all ages and occupations. Developing AWE is the single biggest factor in determining whether you plateau or continue on to reach the highest levels of success.

I found my calling because someone was kind enough and strong enough to tell me that I wasn't as good as I thought I was. If I were to attend a symphony, I wouldn't know that the violin was off key, but when it comes to human interaction, I have perfect pitch. If it hadn't been for Turner Smith, I might have spent my whole life as a mediocre lawyer instead of a damn good agent. We need more Turner Smiths and Alfred Gellers in our lives, people who are willing to tell it to us straight, to force us to take a hard look at our strengths and weaknesses, and to guide us as we work to improve. But even if they recognize the importance of strong AWE, very few people in your orbit will have the guts to honestly tell you when you're lacking in authority, warmth, or energy. I wrote this book to fill that gap. You're about to learn a foolproof way to become a better communicator, make a better impression, build more trust, and draw more people to you. It's those skills that will make the difference between a life spent in the middle and a life at the top. In my experience, it's the person brave enough to do the self-analysis this exercise requires, and determined enough to put in the work to improve, who is favored to win.

My bet is on you.

| # WHAT'S BLOCKING YOU?

Gus got to the bar first and grabbed his favorite table in the corner, sitting with his back against the wall so his friend Emilio would easily spot him when he walked in. As he took his first sip of beer, he thought about how long he and Emilio had been meeting here. They had found it twenty-five years ago, at the end of a long day that they had begun by emptying out the apartment they'd shared while pursuing their MBAs, packing up their lives in a yellow moving van, and moving to the city. The bartender had mistaken them for brothers. With their similar build and coloring, it hadn't been the first or last time. Their lives had followed parallel paths ever since. Both had landed positions as assistant brand managers at a global company. Both had proven themselves to be intelligent and hardworking, and were well liked among their colleagues. Both were happily married to equally intelligent, hardworking women and were raising terrific kids. Both had risen up the corporate ranks roughly around the same time. In the past few years, however, their careers had diverged. Gus had changed jobs and companies multiple times in pursuit of the pay raises and promotions he knew he deserved. His current position was a good fit, and over the last three years, during which he had brought in some lucrative customers, he had regularly earned positive reviews from his boss and his team. "Keep up the good work," his boss had said during his last 360. He was optimistic that this, finally, was where he would be allowed to show his leadership chops and truly shine. It sure was taking a long time, though. Meanwhile, Emilio had continued his steady rise at the same firm that had trained and molded him, taking on bigger and bigger management roles before he'd finally been lured away with a sweet package to work for the number one competitor in the field. Tonight they were celebrating his recent promotion to senior vice president of global operations.

Finally, the door opened and Gus saw Emilio step in. His eyes quickly scanned the room, then locked in on his buddy sitting in the back. Gus raised his glass in a salute, smiling, but as he watched Emilio make his way to the bar to order his drink, he felt his stomach tighten a little. What the hell was that? Jealousy? He was happy for his friend, really he was. Still, he couldn't help but wonder, why him and not me?

Emilio slid into his chair, his scotch sloshing a little as he set it on the table. Gus held up his glass.

"All hail the conquering hero!"

Emilio grinned. "Shut up. No, seriously, thanks."

"Your days must be packed. You barely had time to breathe before; what's it like now?"

"Not so bad. I'm mean I'm busy, don't get me wrong, and the days are long, but I've got a terrific team under me who—"

"Janet still there?"

"Yes, Janet is someone I talk to a lot about—"

"Janet and I worked together back at PMI. She could command a room like nobody's business. I'm not surprised she's there. I should look her up."

"Yeah, she's great. She was actually with me in Augusta when—"

"Augusta for the Masters?"

"Yes, we—"

"You went to the Masters?"

Emilio grinned. "I did. It was insane. You ever been on a private plane?"

Gus took a sip of his beer before replying. "Uh, no."

"I'd never pay for it myself but I can't lie, it's a great way to travel. And you should see the company hospitality headquarters. They built these huge, gorgeous homes—"

"Yeah, I've heard about those."

"Yeah, they're beautiful. Lady Antebellum performed on—"

"Jenny started listening to them a long time ago and I didn't really get it, but we went to see them about two years ago and they were incredible. Good show."

An awkward silence descended over the table until Gus said, "Dude, I'm happy for you. Maybe one day my company will send me to the Masters, too."

Emilio looked at Gus sympathetically. "Hey, don't sweat it. You'll see, you'll be next."

Gus made a face. "I don't know. I've been there awhile now. They keep telling me I need to bring in more business, better clients. But I brought in that big account I told you about last year. What else am I supposed to do? I'm doing the best I can, you know?"

Emilio shrugged. "Totally. You're doing great. If they don't see how much value you bring, the problem is them, not you. You need to find a company that appreciates you."

Gus nodded into his beer. Emilio was right. It was time to move on again.

LOOK IN THE MIRROR

One could see this as a turning point in Gus's life, a moment where he started getting serious about taking control of his professional life. Not me. As far as I'm concerned, Gus just grounded his career for good because he's got spinach in his teeth and no one has the nerve to tell him. And if, like Gus, you've ticked off all the requisite boxes on your field's checklist for professional advancement, yet seen yourself left behind as your colleagues and competitors zoomed up their career ladders, you've likely got spinach in your teeth, too.

Let me explain. Let's say you prepared for weeks to make an important presentation, the kind where a close-up of your face will be projected on a big screen so everyone can get a good look at you. And let's say that on that big day, when you stood up on the podium and began to speak, you revealed a little bit of leftover lunch—a piece of spinach lodged in between your teeth. You could be the most polished, poised person in the room, and no one would notice. Jewels of wisdom could fall from your lips, and no one would be able to hear them. Why? Because the flash of green they're spotting every time you open your mouth would make it impossible to focus on anything else! Your entire interaction with your audience, in that moment, would be hijacked by an unsightly spot of spinach.

Now, one of the many differences between this book and others about good communication practices is that I make no distinction between public and private speaking. In fact, I believe there is an overrated correlation between public speaking and success, and an underrated correlation between private speaking and success. Any trait, characteristic, or bad habit that unbeknownst to you hampers the effectiveness with which you present yourself or communicate *on a daily basis*, especially at work though not exclusively so, is the equivalent of that unsightly, off-putting bit of spinach. It could be a squeaky voice, a condescending attitude, a sloppy appearance, or a disregard for personal space that makes people uncomfortable. Even a poor handshake or a thick regional accent can prevent people from perceiving you as the superstar you really are. These traits and habits may seem inconsequential, even superficial, but if they keep you from showing yourself off in your best light, block your ideas from being heard and understood, and prevent people from trusting and believing in you, they are getting in the way of your success. In my experience, gleaned from twenty-five years of guiding high-striving talent to the pinnacle of their careers, when all else is essentially equal—education, work ethic, intelligence, experience, ambition—the single biggest factor to winning business, promotions, friendships, followers, and voters comes down to one thing: our ability to communicate and make deep human connections.

My anecdotal evidence is supported by a seminal study published by the prestigious Carnegie Foundation for the Advancement of Teaching that asked participants what factors were the most important in determining probable success or failure in terms of employment and promotion. Its conclusion: only 15 percent of one's financial success is attributable to technical proficiency and knowledge. The much larger influencer of your financial success— the 85 percent—rests on your personality, and your ability to communicate, negotiate, and lead. In a word: your *connectability*.

At first glance, these lopsided percentages might seem dubious, in large part because this study was done in 1918 on a population of 1,500 engineers. If there were one field where you might not expect connectability to be a determining factor of success, it would be engineering, and especially one hundred years ago before the advent of all the communication technology that's transformed billions of us, regardless of our profession, into human megaphones. Yet according to the National Soft Skills Association, the findings of this study, while dated and imperfect, have been replicated by the Carnegie Foundation,

Harvard University, and the Stanford Research Center after extrapolating the data.

The results hold up. Many gatekeepers in the professional world admit that they base a large part of their decision making on the presence or absence of the 85 percent, generally agreeing that nontechnical social skills are essential to workplace success and to reaching one's full potential. In a *Wall Street Journal* survey of nearly 900 executives, 92 percent said soft skills were equally important or more important than technical skills. And a LinkedIn survey of hiring managers revealed that skills like interpersonal communication, teamwork, and a friendly personality were at the top of their list of most sought-after traits. One Harvard paper reports that applicants who demonstrate strong connectability are also offered higher pay.

Even in technical careers such as IT and health care, soft skills are considered "baseline skills," a requirement for the job. Specifically, in the tech industry, which traditionally attracts large numbers of self-proclaimed antisocial programmers and engineers, and where the culture often encourages technical expertise above all else, management and investors are beginning to recognize that the lack of interpersonal skills in their workforce is a weakness and a liability. Google's Project Oxygen, which researched its own pool of top employees since the company was founded in 1998, surprised everyone when it reported that out of the eight qualities considered most important, STEM skills (science, technology, engineering, and math) came in eighth. Absolutely last! Again, hovering at the top were qualities like good communication and empathy. Silicon Valley companies have suggested that their teams' lack of the soft skills that foster connectability has been directly responsible for creating dysfunctional teams and products that don't perform well.

Things get even more problematic when we learn that 63 percent of recent college graduates say they are very prepared in
the soft skills required to be successful at their jobs, but only
14 percent of employers agree. That's a huge gap. Because the
cost of a mis-hire can accrue a significant cost to employers,
many companies are investing more time and capital in "teasing
out" the 85 percent by developing tests and other screening
methods, and introducing training programs. But many aren't.
Which means too many new grads and young employees aren't
being informed when they lack these crucial communication
skills. Often it doesn't matter so much in the early stages of their
career, but that weakness can have an outsize effect later, when
promotions are often based on how much new business a person
brings in or how much confidence they inspire.

You will always be at a professional disadvantage if your
too-soft voice and ducked head make you seem timid, if your
hunched shoulders and rambling, monotone speech convey in-
effectiveness, or if you project aggression and self-consciousness
instead of assertiveness and self-confidence. Remember that
famous scene in the movie *Glengarry Glen Ross* when Alec Baldwin
barks that the secret to sales is "Always be closing"? It turns out
that the most successful people intrinsically understand that all
successful human interactions are a form of selling, and they
follow a similar-sounding mantra—*Always be connecting.* To do
otherwise is to relegate yourself to what I call the vortex of
mediocrity. That's where you're doing the job but you have no
control over the game. As Steven Shapiro, founding partner of
GoldenTree Asset Management and a member of the board of
overseers of the University of Pennsylvania Law School, says,
"We have a saying at the firm: You can buy a pound of brains at
the butcher. I walk through the halls of the university, and there

are many brilliant future lawyers. But they can't look you in the eye in the hallway. In fifteen years, this person may be writing law on the tax code, but they're probably not going to have a lot of clients." You know where lawyers, or salespeople, or consultants go when they don't bring in business?

Neither do I. Because you rarely hear about them ever again.

STYLE OVER SUBSTANCE

I often receive a lot of pushback when I suggest that one's style of connecting and soft skills can get them further in life than their substance. To that I say, you just can't cover up a bad steak with good sauce. But while substance is crucial, it's only a piece of what wins business, promotions, friendships, and followers. The best idea or team member does not always win, because without an effective communication style, you cannot persuade people or leave a strong, positive impression. This is not my rule; systematic research shows that we make our minds up about someone in about seven seconds, with our initial impression based on the person's face in less than one-tenth of a second. Those very first impressions allow us to "thin slice," or quickly assess, another person's behaviors, intentions, beliefs, and values. From there, data shows that our early assessments have a profound impact on professional and personal outcomes—whether we offer or are offered the job, ask someone out on a second date, or vote for a candidate. Understanding that we're each making impressions on people all the time and that these imprints are created almost immediately, how does one make the best snap impression? Can we really control how others perceive us? The answer is definitively YES. And where style and substance are not mutually exclusive, you're more likely to make the best impression with stronger style than substance. That said, if you *only* have style and no substance, you won't be able to fool people for long. (A bad steak, once you cut through the sauce, is a bad steak.) But even if you're incredibly substantive, you'll lose your audience if you're lacking authority, warmth, and energy, what I call AWE. You might not like hearing it, but the truth is that the world *does* judge a book by its cover, so take a look at yours. Is it hurting or helping the hard-won substance within you?

REFOCUS YOUR FOCUS

Look, it's actually great news that 85 percent of your financial success is attributable to your soft skills. Whereas robots can now automate many technical skills and proficiencies, genuine and solid human connection still isn't easy to simulate or outsource, and yet they're applicable to every job function, industry, and level of seniority. Master communicators and connectors set themselves apart in every field. Astrophysicist Neil deGrasse Tyson could have remained another respected research scientist working in a lab, but his passion for science and his gift for explaining complicated topics like subatomic particles and quantum mechanics in funny, familiar terms turned him into a household name whose lectures sell out in theaters around the country. Technically, Deb Perelman's Smitten Kitchen is just another good food blog, but she owes her multiple awards and bestselling author status, plus over a million Instagram followers, to an unpretentious, self-deprecating wit and an uncanny ability to transmit her enthusiasm for every dish in such a way that readers and viewers want to eat it right *now*.

But I'm not like them, you might be thinking. I don't want to be a performer, and I have zero desire to become a celebrity. That's fine, but don't kid yourself. When you're at work, you're being judged on your "performance"—how you execute your job, sure, but also on your overall persona: how well you sell yourself and your ideas, how easily you work with others, how effectively you communicate, how smoothly you resolve conflicts, and how well you anticipate others' needs.

However, there's an important detail to note: Those who excel at these interpersonal skills aren't performing at all—it's second nature. It's authentic. It's how they live their lives. You'll get the same attention and engagement from them whether they're leading you through an important project or you bump into them at the grocery store. To reach a celebrated status within your field or even just within your office takes more than just plain hard work and know-how. It takes charisma, leadership, empathy, deep listening, and confidence—all the "soft skills" no one taught you anything about during your years of higher education or certification. You can develop all of these qualities by maximizing the three key communication traits that, in my experience, human beings respond to the most—AWE. That is, the Authority you exhibit, the Warmth you convey, and the Energy you exude and bring out in others.

AUTHORITY. We know it when we see it. We know it when we hear it. Authority stands up tall. It's competent and commanding. Whether it's delivered softly or loudly, it sounds confident. The most successful salespeople, businesspeople, broadcasters, and politicians—all people—embody authority. Do you?

WARMTH is communicated through humility, vulnerability, empathy, and by your attentiveness, your listening ear. That's because effective connection isn't just about output—projecting your message outwards into the world. Input, how you receive the crowd, group, or single individual you're communicating with, is equally important to making an effective connection.

Warmth is necessary to create trust, as well as relatability, which is crucial to solidifying your position on a team.

ENERGY is communicated through your emotional commitment to your message. When you believe in and trust what you're saying, your audience inevitably will, too. Your emotional commitment makes an emotional connection that can be extremely memorable, impressionable, and persuasive. That doesn't mean you have to always be "on." There are benefits to high and low energy; what matters is how it's communicated and received. When your new date is completely focused on you and making it clear they're interested in you—by making eye contact, for example, and nodding a lot to show they're listening—not only do you feel attended to and warm toward this person, but also you're energized because of their attentiveness. But no matter how hot they are, if they're not attentive and not listening, they will deplete your energy, and you won't be eager to seek out their company again.

There's no one-size-fits-all formula for success, but AWE is a pretty near fit for everyone. There is plenty of overlap that can occur within these categories, and in my experience it's possible to assign any trait to one of them. While you don't necessarily have to excel in all three categories of AWE to be an awe-inspiring connector, you need to be pretty effective in at least two of the three. And if you're tanking in any one of them, you're more than likely tanking in some important area of your life. The bottom line is this: those who fail to see the value in understanding their own weaknesses do so at their own peril. Upping your AWE is not necessarily about bringing down the house by giving the most rousing speech at your best friend's wedding, or at your next meeting or company retreat. Rather, it's about helping you tweak, shift, and swap out your weaknesses or bad habits so you become more compelling, more confidence-inspiring, and more respected than you are now.

Whoever you are and whatever you specialize in, you very likely have the technical competence and basic know-how to get the job done—the 15 percent. Yet even with every degree and extra credential in the world, if you want to stand out from your colleagues, to excel and rise above your competitors, you need to refocus your focus on the 85 percent that will make the biggest difference between where you are now and where you want to be.

It worked for Gus. Gus and Emilio are actually based on real people, friends of mine. Gus was familiar with the AWE vernacular and had expressed interest in my coaching work, so finally one day I decided our forty-year friendship would give me cover to offer an unsolicited observation that could explain why he hadn't seen the same career success as Emilio: Emilio knew how to lay out, and Gus didn't. In sports broadcasting, "laying out" refers to a key point during a game when the announcer doesn't talk, instead letting the action and the pictures or the crowd noises convey the power of the moment. Years ago, it wasn't a common tactic, but now it's standard among young announcers because it's so effective. In this context, it's a well-timed pause, a moment where you show you're interested enough to hear what the other person is thinking.

Gus was authoritative—he was knowledgeable about many things and usually spoke with assurance and confidence. He had good energy, always happy to engage and rarely complacent about anything. But his frequent inability to really listen when people were speaking made him seem indifferent and self-centered. When talking to him, you could see him coiling up to throw out a response before you'd even finished making your point. It felt like you were talking to Interrupting Cow. As in:

"Knock-knock."

"Who's there?"

"Interrupting Cow."

"Interrupting Cow—"

"Moo!"

He was so eager to score, he left little room for anybody else to add to the conversation. He was engaged, but his intensity could be so exhausting it sometimes caused other people to disconnect.

Gus had a perfectly respectable career in middle management, but he had the potential to do much more. I was sure his bad habit of interrupting and overpowering a conversation was contributing to a perceived lack of warmth and was hurting his ability to earn the trust of potential new clients and to bring in the business necessary for gaining the kind of respect and confidence from his bosses that could lead to senior leadership status. Unfortunately, he had been walking around with this piece of spinach in his teeth for forty-seven years, and no one, including me, had ever had the nerve to tell him.

Gus was familiar with my work and had already expressed interest in the AWE concept. He'd even told me that he'd taken to analyzing his colleagues' AWE, or lack thereof, at his company. So when he shared some of the results from a training session to which his company had sent him that specifically (but far too gently) noted that his listening skills had room for improvement, I knew I'd found my opening. Not only did I tell him I could pinpoint the problem, I started interrupting him the same way he interrupted everyone else. As soon as he got a taste of his own medicine and experienced what it was like to be on the receiving end of his interruptions, he understood the problem and was eager to start fixing it. That's what's beautiful about AWE training—with just a little self-awareness, it's simple to digest the problem and easy to implement improvements and adaptations on the fly. True, my long friendship with Gus helped establish a high level of trust, but still, he could have gotten defensive or started resisting my advice. Several paying clients certainly have. But he didn't, and the results were extraordinary. I noticed an improvement in our interactions right away. Our conversations had better flow, and we actually grew closer. I had to believe that if he was making the same effort at work and allowing people to see what a good guy he was, it would have a similar effect on everyone with whom he interacted. Sure enough, it wasn't too long before Gus reported that he'd started acquiring new clients at double the rate of the previous year. Within another year, he finally got the promotion to senior management he'd wanted for so long.

LEAVE NO STONE UNTURNED

You may have heard that our words account for only a tiny fraction of our successful communication through the often quoted "7–38–55 Rule," which claims that 7 percent of communication relies on spoken words, 38 percent relies on voice, and 55 percent relies on body language. It's not true. That rule has been widely misinterpreted to refer to all forms of communication, when in fact it is only relevant with regards to communication of attitudes and feelings. Yet how we speak does matter as much as what we say. Andres Varón can attest to that. Born in Mexico, he moved to the United States in his mid-twenties to pursue a PhD in economics from Harvard. Afterward, he worked for multiple banks, eventually landing a high-ranking position at a well-known one. But one day when I asked him how things were going at work, he admitted frustration. By all standards he was doing extremely well, yet he still felt like a worker bee. He wanted to be the one making deals. I hesitated. I thought I knew what the problem might be, but I wasn't sure how my friend would take it.

At issue, I believed, was his beautiful, thick Spanish accent. Despite all his years living in the States, his accent frequently made it hard for Americans to understand him. And I was sure that when competing in a U.S. market, it was undermining his Authority. I decided to take the risk. If he took steps to soften his accent, I suggested, it might make a difference in how the top brass at the company perceived him. To my relief, he didn't take offense. Instead, he signed up for accent reduction classes with the renowned speech therapist Sam Chwat, also known as "Henry Higgins to the stars." Perhaps a year later, he was recruited by one of the world's largest financial advisory groups, where he is now managing director of their Mexico division.

Let me be clear: I wasn't criticizing Andres's accent. If he had asked a woman out on a date and she'd turned him down because of his nationality or accent, I would have thought good riddance, he deserved someone who appreciated him exactly as he was. But we were talking about work. If you're not happy with where your career is going and are determined to do better, it won't help you to shy away from facing reality. You have to be unsparing in your critique and ask yourself, what are the variables keeping me from making myself indispensable to the success and growth of my company?

Is it that you don't have the right education?

Is it that you don't work hard enough?

Is it that you don't work well with others?

Is it that you don't have enough experience?

Is it that there is tension or conflict between you and your boss or other superiors?

If you dig deep within yourself and the honest answer to all of these questions is still "no," you're left with only a few other possibilities. And if you have a thick accent, a squeaky voice, a slouch, or any other trait or habit that weakens your authority, that's one of them.

I asked Andres if he was at all offended by my suggestion that he'd get further ahead if he worked on his accent. Did it feel like he was being asked to deny his ethnicity or conform to Anglo standards of "acceptability"? He was emphatic. "No, because I knew I had an accent. I've always been very critical of myself, so I took it as a constructive comment that I knew I could improve upon." He hadn't been able to immerse himself in American culture at a young age growing up, and he knew it hampered him in more ways than just the way he spoke. For example, he had a hard time getting certain jokes and cultural references. Who the heck was Mr. Rogers? He understood that in order to be successful in this culture, he needed to be able to speak as fluidly in English as he could in Spanish. In fact, he made the point that accent reduction classes weren't really enough. At the very least, he figured it couldn't hurt.

There is no shame for wanting to change or improve something about yourself that is holding you back from exploring the limits of your potential and success. Ask Ralph Lifshitz, who became Ralph Lauren because it's not easy going through life with the word "shit" in one's name (not because he wanted to erase any trace of his Jewish ethnicity). Or Lucille Ball, whose career sparked after she transformed herself from a brunette to a redhead. If you could, you might go back in time and ask England's King George VI how working with a speech therapist to diminish his strong stutter helped him inspire confidence and courage in his people during World War II.

Self-awareness is one key ingredient to finding your AWE, but another is unflinching pragmatism and a willingness to face the world as it is, not lament what it should be. Should it matter what you look or sound like? No. Should we be judged exclusively on the breadth of our knowledge and the extent of our experience? Yes. But like it or not, how we look, sound, and hold ourselves influences how much others are inclined to follow us. We see it in politics all the time, when voters reject the individual with the most experience and clear-cut expertise in governing or policy in favor of someone they "like." Every career move you make, whether you're a librarian or a CEO, is a political play in miniature.

AWE IS IN THE EYE OF THE BEHOLDER

The reality is that historically, by and large it is white men who have set the standard for what constitutes ideal levels of Authority, Warmth, and Energy, and how those traits should manifest themselves in candidates vying for promotion and recognition. By some estimates, 85 percent of all jobs are found through networking, which can be problematic when "'who you know' often mirrors 'who you look like'" or where you come from. Though many companies are working hard to build more inclusive, supportive cultures, it can admittedly be much harder for women and men and women of color to break into senior and executive positions.

That discrimination, injustice, and barriers to diversity still exist in the workplace is unfair. But solving those problems is not the scope of this book. I'm not qualified to address them. What I am qualified to do is help you boost your career and improve your life at this particular moment in time. If you believe a lack of diversity in your workplace or field could be responsible for your career stagnation, you might feel compelled to fight the system and work toward a better tomorrow. Good. But that doesn't have to preclude *you* from doing what it takes to get ahead in the world as it exists today. You don't have to erase what makes you unique or different to benefit from the strategies in this book. Rather, you can use these strategies to emphasize how your unique or different perspective is a part of what makes you excellent and valuable to a company. I'm not saying you won't excel and earn the positions you want if you disregard my advice. It's simply a matter of giving yourself better odds of finally becoming a gatekeeper, which may be one of the fastest ways to remake the world as it should be.

Not everyone will respond to your AWE exactly the same way. Part of being AWEsome, then, is to notice when our attempts at Authority, Warmth, or Energy don't quite hit the mark, or even make someone uncomfortable. Again, it's not about tamping down who we are, it's about being empathetic and respectful enough to care about other people's feelings, and working to figure out how best to connect with them in a productive, positive way.

If you're happy with how things are going at work, the techniques in this book can help bolster the success you have achieved thus far. If you're frustrated and you want to consider all avenues to fulfilling your professional potential, the answer could be here. Your lack of AWE could be the piece of spinach that has been hurting your career for years. And the best way to overcome a problem is to eliminate it. With a little self-awareness and repetitive practice, you can dramatically improve your AWE and create a totally new impression on those who hold the keys to your advancement, as well as your team and colleagues.

When you're getting the accolades and the thumbs-up, the

promises and optimistic predictions, but not the actual promotions, you're not as good as you need to be. Something is lacking. Perhaps you've done your best, or at least what you think is your best. There are very few people on this earth who are reaching their potential. Deep down you know you have two or three more gears to give. Let's figure out what's holding you back and get you to hit it. While you may never get a second chance to make a good first impression, you'll never have a better chance to improve your impression than the present moment. It's not too late to become AWEsome.

I'm here to help you see what your best really looks like. Once you've got clarity, you'll be in a stronger position to embrace and improve your AWE, getting you closer to that life you always had in mind.

Now, if you got in your car and noticed in the rearview mirror that all day you'd been flashing a glob of green stuff every time you smiled, what's the first thing that would run through your head?

Why didn't anyone tell me?

The answer to that is the same one that explains why society has conspired to keep you from getting the necessary feedback you need to make the leap from good to great.

| # THE PROBLEM WITH YES

In the 1990s one of the best players in basketball was the charismatic center Dikembe Mutombo, a relatively lithe, seven-foot-two smiling gentle giant. The best and most salient part of his game was his shot-blocking ability. Mutombo would dare opposing players to enter his domain under the basket and forcefully swat away their attempts, each time punctuating the blocked shot by wagging his index finger to both his opponent and the crowd, as if to underline his unspoken threat, "Not in my house." When Mutombo wagged his finger, there was no subtlety, no question—you'd been *rejected*!

In the game of basketball, coming up short is an obvious loss. But for most of us who aren't professional athletes, the signs that we aren't performing at the top of our game and might be at risk of missing our goals are a lot less obvious. Unlike in sports, where there are clear winners and losers, and where coaches immediately point out mistakes and rarely compliment or inflate their players' performance, in the real world there aren't many people willing to lean forward like Turner Smith or Dikembe Mutombo and throw you out. Why? Because we live in a society that has done its best to convince you that you can't take criticism or rejection, and worse, has taken steps to make sure you never have to.

Early on in my career I interviewed a news reporter from Columbus, Ohio. He had a solid on-air résumé reel; he'd reported on every story from government corruption to presidential elections and everything in between. In addition, he had a closet full of local Emmy awards, an achievement he punctuated in our meeting. But these rewards weren't enough, he admitted. Even with all his accolades, his career wasn't yet where he wanted it to be. He was frustrated that, for all his achievement in the industry, he had been repeatedly passed over for the lead anchor position, a goal he'd worked toward his whole career. He was baffled by this. What was blocking his success? I leaned forward.

"Every year you get these trophies," I said, "but your news director won't give you the promotion you want. Doesn't make sense."

"Exactly," he said, nodding in agreement.

I continued. "You know, in the local news market, it's kind of a running joke that everyone—at least, if you stay in the business long enough—gets an Emmy."

He looked at me blankly.

"If everyone's winning," I continued, "how do you know who's really standing out from the rest?"

He hesitated.

I forged on. "You're receiving praise from your colleagues in the industry, but that feedback is a fiction. You're clearly not a winner yet."

"What do you mean," he challenged, "clearly *not* a winner?"

"Why aren't you getting the promotion?" I asked. "My guess is that you're not receiving a truly honest assessment of your performance. If you want the lead anchor gig, you need to find out what you're doing wrong."

Like my client, if you joined the U.S. workforce any time within the last thirty years, you have probably rarely gotten the feedback you need, and you have likely grown accustomed to getting more praise than you deserve. This reporter had been affected by three forces conspiring to inflate his ego and appease his hunger to excel. Being aware of these forces will speed up your ability to take steps to limit their effects on you.

1. **TROPHY CULTURE:** The other day I bumped into my six-year-old neighbor as he was returning home from a chess tournament. Beaming, he clutched in his hand a shiny three-foot-high red and gold trophy. I congratulated him and asked how it felt to come in first place. "I didn't win first place," he replied. "I won second!" You'd think I'd be used to it by now—I have kids of my own, one of whom played on a youth basketball team where, regardless of ability, interest, and effort, every kid leaves the court with a reward, in the form of a sticker or a ball, for showing up—but I was still taken aback. A three-foot-high trophy for second place? For a six-year-old? What the heck was he going to expect if he won first place at age sixteen—a car?

We all know how the self-esteem movement of the late 1980s and '90s buried us in a mountain of plastic figurines, ribbons, and stickers that got handed out to every child on every team and to every participant at every school science fair, regardless of how well or poorly they prepared and performed. It's gotten to the point that for some students, the value of trophies has been diminished to "party favors: reminders of an experience, not tokens of true achievement." One could argue that there's little harm in making sure the less athletic kids on a team or the students with less parental support at school don't feel ignored or left out. I get it. I was the slow, pudgy kid who was made fun of and sometimes got stuck in right field. The shortstop got the trophy, I did not. I know how it feels. And we should find ways to honor the kid who guts it out even when the odds are stacked against her or when she bravely steps up to a challenge. Unfortunately, what might have started out as a way of sparing a young child's feelings in competitive arenas has morphed into a near-universal habit of rewarding mediocrity with a false sense of excellence, one that has spread far beyond the Little League field. For example, over the course of my adult life, I've been up and down the scale with Weight Watchers. And while the points system has helped me shed many unwanted pounds, I've never agreed with their praise system. No matter whether a person loses a pound or ten, makes no progress at all, or even goes up a pant size in the week preceding the last weigh-in, EVERYONE gets a star. That's right, every single person who gets on the scale receives a round of applause. Irrespective of achievement, the reward is the same. It's not that we shouldn't be happy when someone who wants to lose weight manages to lose a pound, but when everyone receives equal amounts of praise for effort, it dilutes true accomplishment.

Regardless of how we got here—whether through an overdose of GenX political correctness or Millennial oversensitivity—it's time to toughen up. We shouldn't *want* praise unless we know we've put in the work to truly deserve it.

2. **GRADE INFLATION.** Grade inflation is a natural extension of trophy culture. Between the implementation of high-stakes standardized testing that ties public school funding to test scores, and the incentives for elite or expensive schools to be able to advertise high acceptance rates to selective universities, grade inflation is rampant (most significantly at private independent nonreligious schools). An "A" simply doesn't mean what it used to. An investigation of forty-four states revealed that a vast majority of public two- and four-year colleges enroll more than a half a million unqualified students each year. To break that down, that's about one in four kids who show up in the fall but aren't ready for college-level work. More important—because they've been promoted with their peers despite not having met academic performance standards, because they've been allowed to retake tests and complete makeup work and do anything and everything to raise their grades even when they haven't learned the material, and for some, famously, because their parents paid to cheat the system—they're unaccustomed to academic failure.

But it's not in college where they'll get their first taste of it. Faced with having to get record numbers of students up to speed, and unwilling to fail degree candidates, many academic institutions have attempted to fix the problem by perpetuating it: they've lowered their standards and inflated their averages. Not only do today's college students get more passing grades, but more students are rewarded with exceptional grades. According to a study that analyzed seventy years of transcript records from more than four hundred schools, the A is now the prevailing grade at many colleges and three times more common than it was in 1960. Through no real fault of their own, college students have learned to expect high marks for requisite work. The problem is that bestowing high As on undeserving students is not only a disservice to the students who busted their butts to learn the material or complete their requirements on time, but also makes students ill-equipped to handle rejection of any kind, creating future workers who resist constructive feedback and engaging in objective self-assessment.

Let's pause for a moment. My guess is that you don't believe that the statistics I've listed above include you. You worked hard in school, passed your college prep courses (and even took on a few challenging Advanced Placement classes), graduated on time with all the requisite twenty-eight credits and were accepted to a four-year college with honors. You went on to receive a prestigious degree and perhaps even a postgraduate degree. You did it. You earned it. You're a success. Congratulations.

But what might it mean for you if over the course of your many years in school, work that was at one time considered in the C or B range has been promoted to the superlative A? What if, unbeknown to you, both the mediocre and exceptional students in your school or school district were at some point lumped together and regarded equally as the same? Or if the university you attended awarded As to the general student body, even those who hadn't really earned them, because they wanted the exceptional brand name to carry the day? Even if *you* feel certain that you're not—or were not—a student who was given a pass or an inflated grade for your achievements, what might it mean for you if standards of proficiency and progress were lowered for *everyone*? If the definition of success has been dumbed down, even incrementally, to allow for every-one to succeed, does this affect how you define your own success today?

When you start to chew on all these factors, there's no real way for you to know the true value of your performance, is there? Isn't it possible you have wound up in the workforce with a completely inaccurate sense of your capabilities and achievements? How can you know for sure that you're as good as you think you are—especially when you learn that there's a third force blocking your ability to get an accurate read on your skills and ability?

3. **LITIGIOUS WORK ENVIRONMENTS.** Fifteen years ago or so, my clients used to get fired before they came to me. They don't anymore. They get downsized or laid off. Their contracts aren't renewed. They're vic-tims of a reorg. They've been made redundant. Career coach Dan Miller invited readers of his blog *48 Days* to submit some of the creative ways they were told they'd been terminated from their jobs: "Released to the marketplace to better achieve your goals." "Transferred." "Evolved." One woman was assured she was being neither terminated nor laid off, it was just that her scheduled work hours "were being reduced to zero."

What's that all about? Companies playing defense, that's what. Work-place lawsuits are expensive to resolve and can be a PR nightmare, so organizations do everything they can to protect themselves from charges of discrimination or otherwise unfair treatment by making sure they never fire anyone. While this is problematic for anyone seeking honest perfor-mance evaluations, in particular it means that in environments dominated by white men—which is most of them—women, and men and women of color, sometimes get even less of the feedback they need than their white male counterparts, out of managers' fear of having "their motives misconstrued," although Sylvia Ann Hewlett's research shows that in reality, any assessment specifically on appearance, dress, or speech, even minority-to-minority, is inherently "emotionally fraught" and "dicey terrain." Unfortunately, this pattern of avoidance cements the status quo and prevents many brilliant, accomplished professionals of all backgrounds and ethnicities from getting the feedback that would allow them to reach the professional heights they should.

But what about coaching? Lots of organizations point to coaching as proof they are a kinder, gentler work environment. And isn't part of the role of a supervisor or HR department to conduct performance evaluations and then work with the employee to shore up their weaknesses? On paper, maybe. In reality, many HR professionals won't tell you what issues or problems surround your performance or how your manager feels about you. It's too risky. As the head of HR of a major telecommunications company once told me, employees who need coaching are usually being "coached out." The formal performance improvement plan (PIP) is often code for "You might want to start looking for a new job," and still, many employers wait too long to terminate employees who aren't performing up to par. Note: just because you're keeping your job doesn't mean you're excelling. In addition, it takes a certain skill set to be an effective coach, and many supervisors don't have it. They certainly don't feel like they have the time to do it, or at least to do it to the extent some employees might need to perform their best. And so they let their employees go with the equivalent of "It's not you, it's me," dooming the employee to repeat the same mistakes over and over.

I saw this in person when I was called in by a midsize organization's director to coach a senior executive whom we'll call Ina. She was a hard worker and competently executed the technical aspects of her job, such as making investment risk analyses and overseeing the brokerage unit. The problem was in her delivery of the work. Her job was to make investment recommendations, but when it came time to present her data and conclusions, she communicated her opinions with such a flat expression, and so little conviction and authority, that no one, not the CEO, the CFO, or the risk management team, felt compelled to trust her judgment. Millions of dollars were at stake. They needed to believe that she believed in her recommendations, but she made no effort to connect emotionally. Without A or W—Authority or Warmth—she couldn't win the room.

There is no reason to think Ina couldn't have improved if she'd wanted to. She just had an important job and a million things on her mind. Smiling and connecting with her "audience," or learning to speak succinctly with energy and confidence, just wasn't a priority. What did that have to do with the quality of her work, anyway? Unfortunately, neither of her bosses—the CEO and the CFO—had bothered to tell her that they were dissatisfied with her performance, and she took their silence as a "yes." She accepted HR's offer for coaching because she knew she was supposed to, not because she wanted to. Had her bosses explained what was at stake, I'm sure she would have taken our training more seriously. As far as she knew, I was the equivalent of a continuing education opportunity. Without understanding the urgency of the situation, she resented the time she had to spend with me, resisted my advice, and made no effort to change. I couldn't blame her. Why should she? From her perspective, everything was fine, and I was a nuisance cutting into her precious work time. After spending a significant amount of time with her in a relaxed environment, I came to believe that her investment ideas were solid. But I had to use a lot of empathy and time to get there, something she wasn't going to get from her bosses.

I approached the HR director and explained that someone needed to tell Ina the truth, that she had six months to improve or she was going to lose her job. By that time, however, the HR director had tired of spending money on something that was producing no results and earning her no reward. Within a year, Ina got her pink slip without ever learning the real reason why she was being let go. She probably thought she'd been a victim of a unit reorganization that made her position superfluous, when in reality she'd been a sitting duck all along. Unfortunately, the company's refusal to be straight with her meant that she took her uninspiring, unauthoritative ways along with her when she moved on. I've always wondered how she fared at her next position.

Ina was great at the 15 percent—the technical proficiency and knowledge necessary to do her job. But she was failing at the other 85 percent—the connectability. As far as I'm concerned, the failure wasn't hers, it was her company's. Her bosses didn't care enough to give her an honest assessment of her performance, and her HR director didn't have the nerve, or maybe the interest or incentive. The whole story illustrates the truth behind one of the most famous lines written by the late Zig Ziglar, one of America's most beloved salesmen and motivational speakers: "Your attitude, not your aptitude, will determine your altitude." You could be the best in your field, but if you can't communicate your work and your knowledge properly, people will never know it, and they won't turn to you when they need someone with your skill set.

Consider this: Without a forthright diagnosis from your doctor or the proper screening for diseases that can fly under the radar, how can you know what's making you sick and how to treat it in time? The most dangerous diseases, such as pancreatic cancer, have a low survival rate, not necessarily because they're inherently more dangerous than other cancerous tumors, but because without the proper screening, they often go undetected.

And by the time it is detected, it's already metastasized and it's too late to treat. This medical metaphor can similarly play out in other areas of our lives. When those in our professional and personal circles withhold honest feedback, we have no clear warning sign that we can, and perhaps *really, really* should, treat what's ailing us. In many cases, had we worked on that ailment, we'd have made a miraculous recovery. But without our attention, a flaw can easily "metastasize" into career mediocrity or worse, perpetual underemployment, underachievement, or full-on unemployment.

THE GRADE INFLATION OF LIFE

Together, mixed messaging, or flat-out omissions, have generally replaced direct dialogue and tough conversations in the workplace and in nearly every space we inhabit, resulting in a lifetime of what negotiator Christopher Voss calls "the counterfeit yes," in which we hear a fuzzy "yes" all while life is actually delivering an all-caps "NO": You didn't get the promotion; you didn't get the sale; you didn't get the girl or guy. We just can't see it because since preschool we've been lulled into a false sense of security where we perceive the absence of constructive or negative feedback as the equivalent to an A. And though ignorance may feel like bliss, the default A works against you.

The grade inflation of life is why you, like my young client in Ohio, are probably not getting the feedback that would otherwise explain why you haven't been able to move your career further. It keeps you stuck in a vortex of mediocrity—unaware of your true strengths, likely unconscious of your weaknesses, and most probably unmotivated to make any significant change that will elevate you out of your plateau.

The self-esteem movement took hold because society decided that it was more helpful and motivating to highlight people's strengths than to illuminate their failings or flaws, that hearing "yes" in any form was more beneficial to an honest "no." It assumed that people were too weak to hear the truth. There was no way to know how my young reporter in Ohio would respond when I pointed out that his career troubles were because he had been on the receiving end of too many counterfeit yesses. Was he insulted? Did he crumble? Of course not. Presented with the opportunity to improve, my client leaned forward in his chair and said, "Thank you." We're not as soft as proponents of the self-esteem movement would like to think we are. We're resilient! We can handle the truth.

At first when my client asked his news director for an honest assessment of why he was passed up year after year for the anchor position, his boss hedged. But when pressed further, he finally admitted, "Okay, you really want to know? It's your voice. It's not a problem when you're reporting live from out in the field. But if you want to sit at the desk, you need to project. You need more audible authority in your voice to lead the newscast."

In this particular case my client worked with a private voice coach and improved his pitch and resonance. Within a year, he was offered a promotion. He turned it down, though, in favor of a terrific new job at a cable news channel.

WHERE DO YOU GO FROM HERE?

How do you raise your own bar if you're not sure where you're falling short? Unless you walk around like former New York City mayor Ed Koch, whose constant refrain was "How'm I doin'?" it could be hard to find out. You're about to learn how some techniques to help identify your weaknesses and better yet, how to fix them, but for now, the best thing you can do to start is:

- Freely admit that you could do better.
- Accept that we live in a culture of grade inflation, where many people in your life aren't likely being forthright about your performance.
- Ask yourself if *you've* been the recipient of counterfeit yesses yourself.
- Recognize that the precursor to making anything you learn in this book work for you is to develop strong self-awareness (a skill we will cover extensively later). Your self-awareness may be your only reliable signal that change or improvement is necessary. When you can't rely on those around you to be forthright, it's time you rely on *you*. Reject the cultural chorus of YES and pledge to hold yourself to higher standards. Be amenable and committed to change.
- If you haven't already, start asking yourself the tough questions: Am I stuck? Have I hit a plateau? Am I disengaged? Have I accepted "good" when deep down I know great is possible? Is there more that I can bring to the table?
- Read between the lines. In all situations, ask yourself: Is this really a yes? Or, is it a counterfeit yes that's really saying, "You could do better"?

The goal of focusing on where you might have failed to do better when you could have isn't to make you feel lousy or dwell on what you haven't accomplished or achieved, or worse, to settle into what Henry David Thoreau famously called a life of "quiet desperation," where you feel a gnawing sense of dissatisfaction and create a void that cannot be filled. Stop yourself before you go there! Don't let "No" mean "never," but rather, "not yet."

AIM HIGHER

No matter how high you've risen or how much praise you've received, there is always room for improvement. Be like legendary newsman Kenny Plotnik, former vice president and news director of WABC-TV, the number one news station in the country, who told me, "When you're number one, you have to continue to turn your head back behind you. Organizations and individuals can easily become complacent and plateau if you don't continue to raise your own bar." Or take Dan Shulman as a role model. From the minute he became the voice of university football and basketball for the Western Mustangs on CHRW radio in London, Ontario, Dan received positive and well-deserved feedback. But still, as he worked his way up the ladder, becoming the voice of the Toronto Blue Jays, then the secondary play-by-play voice for all of NHL hockey, the lead announcer for all of NBA basketball, and, on July 27, 2007, the announcer who called Barry Bonds's 754th home run for ESPN, Dan continued to hold himself to an even higher standard, treating every game like a do-or-die college exam. "As soon as it's over, it's over, and you start prepping for the next game." One of Dan's master prep strategies was to listen to the audio recording of the last game he called. On many occasions when he'd originally thought his "*HOMERUN!*" had also been hit outta the park, he'd humbly conclude after listening to the recording that he could have done better. Dan never became complacent, and I believe his huge popularity and success can be summed up in his own words: "The day you stop trying to get better, you're getting worse."

Are you ready to take a look in the mirror? You might find out you've made some mistakes or acquired some bad habits, but so what? It is always worth the momentary discomfort, disappointment, or embarrassment of recognizing our flaws when we have the opportunity to actually do something about it. You've already proven you have guts—you picked up this book, didn't you? I promise you have just as much resilience. You're ready. No more excuses. Let's get to work.

| # AWE-THORITY PREP

First, enable the voice and video function on your smartphone and record yourself speaking about anything. Literally. I encourage my clients to find any and every excuse to create videos and recordings of themselves. For example, you could ask permission from your colleagues to record yourself in meetings, or at least during interactions in your office. The longer you can keep the recorder rolling, the better. Eventually you will forget that you're being recorded, and you'll drop any self-consciousness so you can see how you really come across to others. You could record birthday greetings for family members, or post videos of yourself on social media and see what kind of response you get. Try memorizing a monologue or famous speech and dictate it while driving around in your car with your phone set to record. Even short snippets and clips will give you a better sense of your natural voice, body language, expressiveness, and energy levels. You have all your waking hours to practice, so use them! Sports stars and lawyers watch recordings of themselves all the time to make sure they're performing at their best. There's no reason why every professional shouldn't do the same.

Second, as you start learning more about AWE, observe others and try to notice where you see and hear the qualities we discuss in these chapters. The first step toward greater self-awareness and making meaningful change is by becoming an acute observer of *others*. By developing a deeper external awareness of

AWE (truly eye-opening), you will then be able to conduct a more accurate and thorough self-assessment (game-changing). To pull a quote from *Mad Men*, "Nobody knows what's wrong with themselves, and everyone else can see it right away." Since we perceive those around us much more clearly than how we see ourselves, start to look and listen for AWE in the people around you. How do they communicate Authority, Warmth, and Energy? Once you develop your eye and ear for effective connectivity and learn how to recognize AWE in all those you observe and interact with, you won't be able to unsee it. Your blinders will be permanently removed and you'll begin to see through the prism of AWE, and eventually turn that beam of light on yourself.

You can also watch YouTube videos of many of the famous people we reference in this book to see and hear for yourself the qualities we have tried to describe.

| # COMMAND AUTHORITY

Authority communicates confidence and conviction. It does not impose, abuse, or exploit. Above all, it inspires. Would England have endured World War II without the stirring oratory of Winston Churchill? Would India have achieved independence without the steely resolve of Mohandas Gandhi? It's nearly impossible to separate the civil rights movement from the influence of Martin Luther King Jr. Every word in his "I Have a Dream" speech draws you in, pulls you along, and makes you understand that he is not merely imagining possibility, but laying out destiny. MLK's authority empowered his supporters and eventually rallied a nation. The same could be said about President Ronald Reagan during his 1987 speech about the Soviet Union. When he commanded then-leader Mikhail Gorbachev, "Tear down this wall!" his resolve was undeniable. With one look, whether during her forceful opening words for the House Judiciary Committee's impeachment hearings of President Nixon, her historic keynote speech at the 1976 Democratic National Convention, or in her immensely popular class at the Lyndon Baines Johnson School of Law, Barbara Jordan commanded respect. When she spoke, people listened.

However, one doesn't have to be a political leader or a civil rights pioneer, or hold a title or even an advanced degree, to communicate authority. Maria Phillipopolous, who until her recent retirement was the proprietor and shoe-fixing doyenne of Dino's shoe repair in Manhattan's Columbus Circle, was proof.

Shoes made Maria happy the way candy brings joy to children. She was like a surgeon who relishes the hardest cases others don't dare to tackle. The walls of her nondescript little shoe shop are festooned with celebrity-signed headshots thanking her for a myriad of shoe-related issues.

Maria is an energetic, confident older woman, probably over seventy, very much a gruff yet loving Greek *yiayia*, a grand-mother. She is small, yet she towered over her store and her customers. When you walked into her store with a problem, she would take the shoe, place it on her counter, and run her hands over it, examining it with the thoroughness of a crime scene investigator. In today's throwaway, fast-fashion culture, you'd have to visit a luxury boutique or artisanal craftsman to witness someone pour themselves into their product or service this way. After nearly four decades in business and a nonstop stream of customers, she had an iron-core confidence in herself and her work, and it showed in the conviction with which she'd finally announce her diagnosis. She'd say it once, in a firm yet loving way, making sure to point out with her rough fingers exactly where the problem lay so you could see for yourself what she was talking about. She conducted her business with such authority and pride, most people didn't even think about questioning her. Should you dare to question her advice or her price, however, she'd go silent. Her stillness, coupled with her steely gaze and erect demeanor, said it all: "I am the best at my job. My store has been here for decades and my customers are demanding. If I've been good enough for their high standards, you're not going to find someone better. Go find someone cheaper. You'll be back." I know what was in her thought bubble because I once made the mistake of going to a shoemaker near my apartment for some new soles. When the shoes were so uncomfortable I considered throwing them out, I sheepishly went to Maria for help. She was immediately angered and wise to my infidelity. "Give me those . . . give me those shoes right now. Just give me those shoes. Take them off!" Rapid and emphatic, her words came out of her mouth like a spray of bullets. She put the shoes on the counter and made me stare at them while she concluded that they'd been incorrectly re-soled. "Okay. Here's your problem. Look at how imbalanced these are," she scolded me, exasperated, pointing out the mistakes made by the offending cobbler who had sullied my shoes and her industry. Before I could atone for my poor choice, she confiscated them. "I will fix them properly," she announced. She did, and I wore the shoes for years.

Maria could read the room and knew her audience. I'd been going to her store for a long time; she knew she could be brutally honest with me. Yet the only difference between the way she spoke to me and the way she spoke to new customers was her tone. She'd say exactly the same thing, and she'd still interrupt you by raising a hand in the air like a traffic cop, daring you to utter another word, but she would do it in a much less brusque, aggressive manner. Regardless, she always controlled the relationship. She made you believe in her. Therein lay her authority.

That's why you need to up this part of your AWE. If you don't believe in yourself, few will believe in your message. That's any message, not just a prepared speech. If you want people to believe that you are as good at your job as you say you are, or believe in a plan you want to implement, or even believe in your vision for a community garden, you must present yourself and communicate with authority. You can have all the expertise or passion for your subject in the world, but if you cannot communicate it with authority, no one in your audience of one to one hundred will hear you, much less believe in you. When you embody authority, people invite you into the discussion and into the room. They trust you, believe you, and are more easily persuaded by your message. A good idea with a weak message often gets lost, dismissed, or entirely ignored. Don't let this happen to you.

Maria may have been an artisan and a small-business owner, but she owed her authority to a command of the exact same skills and qualities as the well-known national and global icons mentioned in the beginning of this chapter. Those skills and qualities are generally expressed through six elements: Voice, Presence, Body Language, Dress, Alignment, and Detachment. Master them all, and mark my words, the people whose respect you hope to earn will notice the difference. Let's break them down.

VOICE

Not many of us can turn a deaf ear. You might not be consciously listening for it, but most of us instinctively recognize authority when we hear it and, contrarily, when it's missing. We all know that person who has an artificially high or singsongy voice and isn't taken seriously, or the speaker with the monotone and mumbled voice who can't hold the room. Where having a good voice is only one variable to communicating with authority, it may be the most important. As legendary voice coach Mort Cooper wrote in *Change Your Voice: Change Your Life*, "Your voice is your second face." Other than your face, nothing else makes a bigger initial impression on people, yet to our detriment most of us don't give our voices the same consideration or "face time." By the time you're done with this chapter, you'll never hear your own voice or anyone else's the same way again.

PPV

The hallmark of authority is communicated through voice via pitch, pace, and volume. PPV, for short. *Pitch* refers to the relative highs and lows of your voice. *Pace* is the rate of speed of your voice. And *volume*, well, you know what that is. With any musical training, you develop an ear for the scales of the instrument you're learning to play. We can each think of our vocal instrument in the same way. We all have the capacity to vary our speech, utilizing a range of notes, rising and falling at different rates and volumes. When we inflect, articulate, and punctuate our speech, we're able to communicate different meaning, and similarly impart a spectrum of attitudes and emotion. If you're a Broadway fan like me, think of the chorus from the opening number of *Fiddler on the Roof*, "Tradition." The lyrics simply repeat the same word—tradition—over and over again with changing PPV. Another song that does this to tremendous effect is Queen's "Bohemian Rhapsody." The element of unpredictability and surprise that is created by varying your pitch, pace, and volume captures your listener's attention and keeps your audience engaged and interested, much like when you listen to a piece of music.

Pitch

Early in my career I had a female client from Staten Island. A marketer, she was extremely frustrated at work. Though she was earnest, intelligent, and hardworking, and cared a great deal about her company, she couldn't seem to get ahead. Her boss didn't respect her; she couldn't convince anyone to give her enough responsibility to prove herself. Now, a voice from Staten Island is distinctive for its singsong quality and an accent that turns "wuds" (words) like "awkward" into "awkwid." This particular Staten Islander had the thickest accent I'd ever heard (and I'm from New York). On top of that, her voice was especially singsongy and could escalate without a moment's notice. Think Joan Cusack in *Working Girl,* with a pitch as high as her character's teased bangs. It was truly extreme, and I was sure that given all her other attributes, her voice and accent were her hidden career killers. My client had just been turned down for a promotion and because I cared about her success, I did my job and suggested she consider voice lessons to soften her accent and lower her pitch. After all, a voice that plays well in Fresh Kills does not always transfer to the boardroom (as Tess McGill, *Working Girl*'s protagonist, quickly figured out). The issue of a too-high pitch seemed like an obvious fix to me because it was such a glaring weakness in her presentation. Surely someone in her life had offered a similar correction at some point? My suggestion landed with a thud. She was appalled and offended. "No one has *ehvaaah* told me that?!" she screeched. "Ehhhvaaaah! Why do you *say* that?" As her voice rose higher and higher, I thought, because I can *hear* it. None of her bosses had ever said anything about her voice and how it might be a liability in a sales-forward position, and she took that to mean I didn't know what I was talking about. We didn't work together long after that. Soon after she rejected my advice, I heard she was "downsized." It's a shame, because she had talent and with the right feedback could have built a strong career. Unfortunately, she thought the absence of a hard "no" meant that her bosses were giving her a "yes," when in fact they were dodging the issue and merely doling out a "counterfeit yes" until she finally took the hint and moved on. I nehvaaah heard from her again.

This anecdote illustrates an extreme case of how a high pitch can weaken a person's authority and professional prospects, but many women will be quick to point out that feminine vocal registers, which are usually higher pitched than men's, in general are often easily dismissed. Beth Mowins, a sports journalist for ESPN, a Susan B. Anthony of play-by-play announcing who not only blazed a trail in the male-dominated field but ascended to the top, says, "What I've heard from male bosses, over the years, is almost a resistance to hear a female voice as being authoritative, along with a long-held belief that a man's voice has to be the lead voice, or a deeper voice has to be the lead voice. That's probably the one thing that I've always either had to fight against or try to work around." Unfortunately, the reality is that there is an undeniable bias toward deeper voices for positions of authority, which has to be infuriating for women and even men whose voices have a naturally high pitch. Some suggest that we associate deeper, more masculine voices with authority because people with lower voices have always had more power. That's certainly a possibility. Another theory is that the bias toward lower-pitched voices doesn't reveal a preference for masculine traits, but for age. As we grow older, theoretically we should be gaining more experience and wisdom, and maybe that's what people subconsciously gravitate toward. Could be. For our purposes, however, the reason most people perceive lower voices as more authoritative is irrelevant. The point is, they do. In fact, researchers have actually established that lower voices seem to confer a professional advantage. In a Duke University study of almost eight hundred male public-company CEOs, the leaders with the lowest voices ran bigger companies, earned more money, and held their positions for longer than men with higher voices. This means that everyone, not just women, needs to be thinking about their pitch.

Pace

Dinnertime in our home was a raucous event. My father was a trial lawyer, my two older brothers would follow in his footsteps, and my younger sister would grow up to get a joint JD/MBA. It was like going into battle to get a word in edgewise, so I learned not to pause when trying to make a point because as soon as I did, I'd get interrupted. The problem is, when you don't stop talking, a) you exhaust your listener and make it hard for them to follow your train of thought, and b) you run out of oxygen. The less oxygen you have, the less you can support your voice and the higher and softer it gets. Not so great when you want to speak in an authoritative pitch, either. Controlling the speed of my speech is something I have to work on all the time.

The best practice for an authoritative pace is to speak in crisp, short, succinct, declarative sentences. Think less is more. Many times, authority is conveyed not by what you say, but by what you don't say. For example, consider your manager's reaction if she were to ask you about the report you're working on and you answered like this:

"The report? Um, yeah, it's coming along! Like, I've got the data, I'm just, like, you know, still fine-tuning some of the numbers and waiting on Henry for a few more details. I mean, like, I should get it to you, maybe like, Friday?"

If you were your boss, would you have any confidence that you were going to see a completed report on your desk by Friday? I'd have serious doubts.

Speaking with authority means learning to be comfortable with silence. Filler words make us sound young and inexperienced. We use filler words to cover for the fact that we're still working through our thoughts even as they come out of our mouths. For some people, it becomes a veritable verbal tic. But it's an easy one to eliminate. The mere act of noticing how many times you insert "uh," "like," or "you know" into your sentences will likely help you cut down the number of filler words in your speech by half. If that doesn't work, try paying attention to how many times other people say it. That's the advice I gave Reid Pakula, a recent college graduate working at our company. From day one, it was evident that Reid was motivated and hungry to succeed. After a month on the job he requested my feedback about how he was doing and whether there was anything he could improve.

I told him, "You use the word 'like' as filler in between words and it undermines your authority. It also makes you sound less intelligent than you are."

Reid was completely unaware of how often he used the word, but committed to using it less. After a few weeks, he asked me if he was getting better. "Not really," I told him honestly. "Try this," I suggested. "Over the weekend don't worry about you saying 'like' but rather listen to the people around you and notice if they say it."

This was the key to Reid's turnaround. He came into work on Monday morning, marched right into my office, and said, "I have some good news and some bad news. The good news is that I will never say the word 'like' again. The bad news is that I cannot stand any of my friends."

This was the turning point. Reid went from external awareness to self-awareness, and now there's hardly a day when I hear the word escape from his lips.

It's okay to pause as you decide what you're going to say. When you deliver your message in a wishy-washy voice or with constant qualifiers and filler words, you undercut your authority and short your success.

Another example of the power of less-is-more was on full display during the first October 2000 debate between George

W. Bush and Al Gore. Gore was without a doubt more versed in substantive policy details than his rival, but Bush's economy of words and strong, crisp answers offset his lack of details and gave him a greater appearance of authority. In trying to show off the depth of his knowledge and understanding, Gore came off as condescending, not authoritative. He knew pretty much everything about, well, everything, and he could substantiate his assertions with hard facts, but no one except policy wonks could keep up with him, or wanted to. (The endless sighs didn't make him look good, either.) He'd hold court for three minutes straight, but the more he tried to sell, the less we wanted to buy (and I liked the guy). Bush may have been considered an intellectual lightweight, but his crisp, succinct speech made people believe in him.

And you wanted to have a beer with him, too.

Establishing authority requires that you know what you're talking about, but lots of people know what they're talking about. You have to communicate it in a way that people can grasp and understand. I know an utterly brilliant oral surgeon, smartest guy you'll ever meet, who has been in practice for years and yet can't seem to grow his business. Why? People come to him to get an opinion on procedures that can cost up to ten thousand dollars. In an effort to help them be informed customers, he'll explain every single detail of every single option that might be available. It sounds something like this: "We could try this technique, but there's a new development that I'm finding very interesting that you could also consider, but then there's a school of thought that this other method is actually the most effective and you might want to consider pulling these four teeth, or I don't know, you could probably get away with only pulling three, but you could pull four, it's up to you." It's like trying to follow the spin cycle in the dryer—you get dizzy. Yes, there may be multiple ways to do a procedure, but at the end of the day, if you're not a dentist, you don't care. You just want your teeth to stop hurting or your smile to look better. Too much choice causes patients a lot of anxiety. They usually wind up choosing an oral surgeon who makes them feel calm and at ease about having someone poke through their mouths with sharp objects. A more authoritative approach would be to help his patients limit their choices. "Hello, Mr. Herz, how ya doin'? Look, there are two ways to do this procedure. I've seen cases like yours ten other times. I've done it this way all ten times. I've had good results all ten times. This is what I think we should do. How does that sound?" Boom. If he did that, he'd have his patients at hello.

This surgeon makes a decent living, but he could do much better. Don't let excessive verbosity cost you business.

Volume

Authority is conveyed through power and confidence, not decibels. There are times when it can be synonymous with volume, of course. When my son was younger, I watched him chase after a ball that rolled into the street just as a car turned the corner. "JACK!" I commanded. He stopped in his tracks and quickly retreated. But think about this: as a child, were you in worse trouble when your dad was hollering, or when he lowered his voice to an angry, tight whisper? As voice coach Ellie Miller says, you don't have to raise your voice to be heard.

Denzel Washington is correct in the movie *American Gangster* when he says, "The loudest one in the room is the weakest one in the room." People may pay attention to someone whose voice is big and booming, but they won't necessarily respect them. We've all seen *that* guy puffing out his chest and speaking to no one in particular. He has a point to make and he's determined to get the last word, the second-to-last word, and the third-to-last word! Where he may be presenting himself as the authority in the room, we can all see through him. He's not an authority; he's a showman.

Yelling is only temporarily effective. It initially grabs people's attention, but if you yell too frequently, people tune you out. It can be scary when an authority figure yells. It's much scarier when an authority figure who never yells, yells.

Communicating authority is not synonymous with volume, but rather with voicing confidence in yourself. Do you believe in what you're saying? When you believe in your message and that you have something of value to give and add to the world, and align that sense of confident authority with your voice, you will command the room. The most authoritative voice can be the most understated.

If you're going to speak, make yourself heard. Finish every sound. Finish every word. Finish every sentence. Put the force of your breath behind your words. Don't trail off, leaving sentences incomplete. Sounding more authoritative really comes down to projecting belief in your own message. If you believe and internalize what you're saying, we will, too.

In sum, the most important thing to remember is that there is no right pace or volume—their appropriate use depends entirely on the circumstances. And while there is such a thing as a wrong pitch—one that is artificially high or low—even a well-placed pitch will become monotone if you don't remember to vary it. Fine-tune your pitch, pace, and volume and you'll see immediate improvement in the way you are received by others. While you're at it, it can be helpful to pay attention to one other vocal quality, as well.

Inflection

We'll talk about inflection more with regards to infusing your speech with energy, but it's tied to authority, too. Inflection refers to the weight you place on words. In both Barbara Jordan's 1974 DNC speech and her delivery at the Nixon impeachment hearings, her gravitas is palpable. From the Nixon hearings, punctuated incorrectly to show how she uses her inflection to incredibly powerful effect:

"My faith in the Constitution is whole it is complete it is total. And I am not going to sit here and be an idle spectator (pause) to the diminution (pause) the subversion (pause) the destruction (pause) of the Constitution."

Not one word is wasted or rushed. There is a slow, methodical, measured quality to her speech, like she's tasting each word before it comes out of her mouth to make sure it's just right. Her voice is powerful and clear, every word supported. Her words never trail off; her pauses are full of meaning. You'll hear the same thing if you listen to Kenneth Feinberg speak. Feinberg, a lawyer, has become known as the go-to guy who handles financial dispensation to victims of terrible tragedies, from 9/11 to Sandy Hook. In his thick Boston accent, he holds your attention with every word he says. You can hear a good example of his authoritative inflection on the episode called "The Tragedy Expert," aired on Alex Blumberg's podcast, *Without Fail*:

He was concerned that if the Vietnam veterans who had suffered SO (pause) as a result of the war *and its aftermath, frankly*, that he was concerned that if there were a trial the Vietnam veterans might very well lose the case.

He wanted the case settled. He wanted SOME SORT of concrete *victory* (pause) for the class of Vietnam veterans who had suffered so, both during the war and after. And he was HOPing that somebody with the, the competence and the political SAVVY (pause) to help negotiate (short pause) a settlement, help mediate a resolution, would be in the best interest of everybody.

To hear Feinberg speak is to hear King Solomon thinking through his judgment out loud.

DRESS

While voice is one of the most powerful communicators of authority, you can also convey authority just by walking into a room.

Legendary basketball coach Frank Mickens became the principal of the Boys and Girls High School in the hardscrabble Bedford-Stuyvesant section of Brooklyn in 1986. He took over a school that was graduating just 24 percent of its students and by the time he retired in 2004, attendance rates soared and the graduation rate nearly doubled to just under 48 percent. How did he do it? Many credit his nonnegotiable insistence on higher standards that extended to the decorum of his students. From his *New York Times* obituary: "Two days a week, the school's 2,000 boys were required to 'dress for success' by wearing a dress shirt and necktie to class. If a student could not afford a tie, Mr. Mickens provided one. The school's 2,500 girls were also required to dress appropriately for success in the working world." Mickens demanded that his students present themselves with external authority, and his results bore out that what they felt on the outside translated to the inside. Their inward confidence pushed them to achieve greater academic heights.

Of course, there's no one-size, "dress for success" that fits all. In every setting, it's important to take into account the culture, current trends, and the general mind-set of your audience. Steve Jobs announcing the iPhone in an ascot wouldn't have worked with his casual, tech crowd. Margaret Thatcher, on the other hand, was famous for her formal attire. Her serious, straight-line suits signaled to her English audience that she meant business. Office workers in hyper-casual Austin can probably get away with a different look than they could in Washington, D.C. (one of the most formal dress codes in the country).

Stephanie Druley, who serves as senior vice president of event and studio production at ESPN and is currently the highest-ranking female employee at the network, makes the point that with wardrobe specifically, our cultural comfort level has changed. The new "look" of authority leans more casual. "In the past," Druley says, "the trend with women in sports was to almost defeminize their wardrobe. It used to be unheard of that you wouldn't wear a jacket with a blouse buttoned up to your neck. But now, women are more comfortable wearing what they would wear off the set. That's a big change."

The Mayo Clinic, as another example, has ditched the white lab coat and scrubs for professional business attire. Their reasoning? They believe that the Mayo uniform, as they refer to it, now worn by all of their physicians, is a visible clue that conveys professionalism and expertise, possibly with the added bonus of minimizing cases of "white coat syndrome," in which patients' anxiety and blood pressure spike at the mere sight of a person in a white lab coat. When administrator of General Service and the Office of Patient Affairs of Mayo Rochester Mary Rogers was just starting out, she worked in a lab where the required dress was a white uniform and white shoes. One day she arrived to work and her supervisor, eying her shoes, demanded that she clean her shoelaces. Mary objected. She didn't work with patients, what did it matter that her shoelaces were a little dingy? Her supervisor explained that every time she set foot outside in her uniform, she was representing the Mayo Clinic, and so she had better look perfect. In an interview twenty-eight years later, Mary said she continued to hold herself to that standard of perfection as a reflection of the level of quality she expected of herself.

Where playing to your audience can make you more relatable, beware of playing a *role*. While he should get credit for his attempt to rebrand himself, especially as his company continues to face hard questions about data privacy and security, many of us just didn't buy it when Mark Zuckerberg, cofounder and CEO of Facebook, started to appear in a suit instead of his predictable, colorless tee and hoodie. Because he's so branded as the casual and aloof Silicon Valley guy, making a change toward a more traditionally authoritative wardrobe seemed to backfire on Zuckerberg. Where in many instances it was perfectly appropriate to the setting to elevate his presentation (when meeting with presidents and prime ministers, for example), still, many perceived his dressing "up" as overcompensation that actually undercut his authority. This doesn't mean you can't evolve, but your authenticity is, hands down, more effective at building credibility and authority than fitting in with the crowd—and this may even extend to appearances before the Senate Commerce Committee.

More important than what you wear and how you present on the outside is what you externalize from within. When you feel comfortable in who you are and allow that certainty to show through, you will be recognized as an authentic authority.

In addition to helping Apple transform from near insolvency to one of the most profitable and recognizable brands in the world, Apple cofounder Steve Jobs understood the value of his own personal presentation. His trademark black turtleneck coupled with his wire-rimmed glasses, blue jeans, and white New Balance sneakers conveyed *relatable* authority. He was the geek turned tech guru to whom many Apple users could relate. Where most in his position of power would present in a suit and tie, Jobs took a unique stand apart from the rest and put his unique twist on the power suit. Independent of Apple's innovative technology, Jobs's signature style elevated him to world-renowned celebrity status. His lavish announcements of new Apple products were more anticipated than most movie premieres, and they were punctuated by his stylistic authority whereby he commanded the stage and the millions of Apple customers who followed online. Jobs understood well the power of outward authority to instill respect and trust and to motivate the masses. Since his passing, Apple has not enjoyed quite the same success or cultural importance absent its charismatic leader.

In every situation, remember who you are, and own it. New England Patriots coach Bill Belichick, no matter the frigid temps, paces the sidelines in his signature grey hoodie, and always with the sleeves cut off. Many point to his defiant and contrarian nature as the reason behind his stylistic approach. He doesn't like being told what to do, or what to wear. He is his own man. Worn game after game and year after year, the sloppy hoodie with the cutoff sleeves has become Belichick's uniform of authority. His insistence to take a stand stylistically communicates confidence, a belief in himself and his own principles. Of course, Bill Belichick can wear a tired-out hoodie and instill confidence in his fans because he's *Bill Belichick*, just as Jerry Seinfeld and David Geffen can garner respect wearing T-shirts and jeans. Will the same wardrobe choices build credibility with your crowd? We can all use stylistic authority to communicate a strong belief in ourselves and our message because it's not so much what you wear as *how* you wear it. Whatever your preferred attire, when you wear your internal confidence on the outside, you will be recognized as an authority. Sleeves or not.

Some would say there is inherent sexism in the fact that a woman could probably never get away with showing up to a board meeting in a hoodie or the same black turtleneck every day. I'm not sure about that. We never see Sheryl Sandberg in a hoodie, but then again, her story isn't consistent with a hoodie. Mark Zuckerberg is a guy who has never worked for anybody else. Jobs was only twenty-one years old when he started Apple Computer. You can wear whatever you want if you're not answering to anyone else. And how you express your authority on the outside often has a lot to do with where you are in your career.

That said, social mores are changing. There are still plenty of industries where formal dress is often required—politics, health care, finance, to name a few—but increasingly, women are rejecting the strictures placed upon them and demanding to be allowed to work in clothing that is comfortable (that is, not high heels), practical, and most of all, real to them. Ultimately, you should wear the clothes and hairstyle that makes you feel powerful and confident. However, good judgment is crucial. Clothes that are too tight, too revealing, or too rumpled distract people from the high performer inside them. Especially if you're someone on the outside looking in on the position or company where you want to be, giving more thought to the way you dress could make all the difference.

An acquaintance, Micah, became a client and good friend when he didn't punch my lights out for suggesting that his choice of dress was hampering his legal career. A former prosecutor in the Manhattan district attorney's office, he's an extraordinarily charismatic, intelligent man, and one of the highest-rated adjunct professors at Cardozo Law School. At the time I met him, he was working at a firm run by some masters-of-the-universe types. Financially, he was doing well, but his professional and social circle was filled with people at the top of their game—professionals, community leaders, and philanthropists whose work was unparalleled. It could be stressful, and it highlighted his frustration at work. He had no equity interest in the firm, and he hated feeling like he was in a dead-end situation. By most standards it was a good dead end, but still, he wanted to feel as engaged at work as he did in his personal life, where he felt like he was pouring the best of his gift and talents. Professionally, he felt capable of more.

As soon as I met him, I could tell, to use baseball parlance, that he was a .350 hitter who was only hitting .260. Part of his problem at work, I was sure, was his look. A heavyset man, he wore the same thing to work every day: a suit, an oxford, and underneath, a ratty white T-shirt. You could actually see the frayed T-shirt collar. He was a criminal lawyer asking people to put their lives and futures in his hands, and he didn't look the part. He looked like Lou Grant. Or an unmade bed.

Micah was open to the critique. "You know what? I'll get new T-shirts."

"No," I said, "No. No. No. That's not the look of a professional. No more T-shirts. Time for a change."

Micah stopped wearing the T-shirts and actually changed his teaching wardrobe altogether, trading out the rumpled suits for a blazer and jeans, a look he'd previously thought "seemed too hip" for someone like him. He also lost some weight and upgraded his haircut. In the time since that physical transformation, he started his own law firm. He recently settled the biggest case of his career, with a huge payout.

Was it really the change in dress that changed everything? He seems to think so. "I always put [fashion] on the back burner because people seemed so obsessed with it. It's almost like you gave me permission to care. Caring about that led to more growth." Micah admits his new look made him feel like he had a "cool vibe, like I could own the room." He felt more confident, which surely had a calming effect on potential clients and made them more inclined to trust him with their cases. As he signed more clients, his confidence grew even more. Word of mouth grew and more people send him referrals. More clients meant more cases and more chances to win, which meant more and bigger clients. One small change in your presence can have a transformative domino effect.

BODY LANGUAGE

It doesn't matter how you dress: if you don't know what you're doing and don't present yourself with authority, you won't garner respect. Example: In addition to his equally distinguishable and relatable look, Steve Jobs wore other outward expressions of authority: upright posture, open body language, and a commanding gait. His presentation on and off the stage communicated absolute conviction in what he was selling—Apple products and himself.

What does authoritative body language look like?

- Open-handed gestures above the waist or even shoulders; gestures below the hips convey weakness. Keep these movements natural, though. Overly practiced gestures will make you look like you're trying too hard.
- Tall, straight posture, whether standing, sitting, or walking, achieved by engaging your core muscles.
- Neck and head held high—think of a wire attached at the crown holding your head straight up.

- Shoulders back—raise your shoulders to your ears, then roll them back and down until they rest comfortably.
- Arms comfortably at sides or resting on hips, not crossed.

PRESENCE

Authority is communicated audibly through voice and outwardly through dress and presentation. It can also be delivered quite potently through one's general vibe.

Once again, confidence plays a big role in determining what kind of presence we exude. Presence refers to a person's physicality, the very way they're built and how it makes people around them feel. For example, club bouncers. Most of the time, they're not getting into fights trying to keep the unwanteds out of the establishment; their mere presence as a six-foot-four, 260-pound piece of granite does their job for them.

A strong presence can be a powerful tool when negotiating, establishing your cred, or dealing with crises or disagreements. Clarissa Ward, the London-based chief international correspondent for CNN, is a modern-day Wonder Woman by many people's assessment, and has been called the "biggest badass in cable news." She embodies a measured authority that emanates from within and doesn't insist on being heard. Rather, it reveals itself subtly and powerfully. Ward believes that her tempered approach is what gives her the authoritative edge she needs to "extract" information from difficult subjects who aren't often willing to engage or reveal themselves.

"When I've interviewed vile jihadists who espouse an ideology that I think is fundamentally evil, the temptation is to get into a kind of fight with them or an argument where you're both raising your voices. I learned that the minute I lose my temper and start fighting, I'd lose the battle and the interview. The way you convey authority is by *not* allowing yourself to get riled up, by forcing yourself to be still, to listen to what they're saying. If I can just keep my cool and keep pressing and asking the tough questions, then *that* to me conveys greater authority and greater command of a subject or a situation than someone who needs to throw their weight around. You want to be in control, whether that's an interview for *60 Minutes* or whether it's talking to someone at a conference, at a dinner party, or at work."

We can look to the third debate between Al Gore and George Bush for another example of how grace under pressure translates to authority. After Gore replied in typical long-winded fashion to a question about a national patients' bill of rights, moderator Jim Lehrer turned to Bush and asked, "I'd like to know how you see the differences between the two of you." Bush replied, "Well, the difference is that I can get it done." Boom. The audience laughed. Bush continued: "That I can get something positive done on behalf of the people. That's what the question in this campaign is about." As he spoke, Gore left his stool and stalked over to Bush's side. Bush, who either didn't notice or was doing a masterful job of ignoring his opponent, continued speaking straight to the audience. "It's not only what's your philosophy and what's your position on issues, but can you get things done."

He looked over at Gore, offering a short, nonplussed nod as if to say, "How ya' doin'?" The audience laughed. Then he turned his head back to the audience and delivered his final message. "And I believe I can." More laughter from the audience.

Maybe Gore was the more qualified candidate. In this moment, it didn't really matter. Bush showed a masterful ability to convey authority through both his crisp, direct speech and calm, unflappable demeanor. Gore, on the other hand, came off as an insecure bully.

People with authoritative presence are unflappable and impeccably respectful, no matter who they're speaking to. Is that you?

ALIGNMENT

When you combine measured authority with the ability to align yourself with your audience, people's perception of and respect for your authority rises even more. The most successful leaders, influencers, teachers, and employers describe a working relationship where the traditional top-down boss-to-subordinate or teacher-to-pupil relationship is replaced with peer-to-peer alignment. Where it's well understood that one person in the relationship is the authority on a subject or within an organization, for example, he or she isn't the acting superior, but rather a *guide*. Instruction isn't pedagogical, but collaborative.

When you communicate that you aren't just in it for yourself, but are in it *with* the person you're coaching, teaching, supervising, or leading, you can exercise your authority to inspire and motivate your team, class, staff, or audience forward. Alignment creates generous room for the exchange of ideas, collaboration and reciprocal guidance toward a mutually beneficial outcome. Dr. Robert Goldstein is an eminently successful anesthesiologist and the founder and chief medical officer of Somnia, a sprawling anesthesia outsourcing company based in Harrison, New York. By his own admission, Dr. Goldstein will tell you he's a decent enough doctor, on the bell curve of having the 15 percent, but that his technical skills have little to do with his success. After struggling with the arduous requirements of the premed program at Michigan State University medical school, he took a one-year leave of absence before resuming his medical studies at the SUNY Downstate Medical Center in Brooklyn. From there he dug in and wound up doing his residency at Yale, eventually becoming a board-certified and licensed anesthesiologist, but he says his esteemed degree only got him a seat at the table. How Dr. Goldstein eventually positioned himself at the head of a multimillion-dollar business and in the top one-tenth of 1 percent in a field littered with medical professionals of equal, or even more, technical talent is a matter of how well he employs his 85 percent. He has a confident, easy charm that he maximizes to build solid connections and navigate relationships with everyone in his orbit.

"It's true that I wasn't the most qualified student applying for medical school," says Goldstein, "but understanding the importance of making connections has guided me my entire life and has been the differentiator for me as a doctor and a businessman."

Where being a doctor gives you that initial credibility, from there you have to align yourself with your patients. The prototypical physician who's the smartest guy in the room turns them off pretty quickly. In Goldstein's experience, patients are typically more impressed by bedside manner—the 85 percent—than a doctor's medical background.

"And there's subjective data that proves that the ability to genuinely connect to others produces the most successful outcome," he says. "Malpractice cases, for example, decrease when patients feel connected to their doctor. And there was an anesthesiology study called the Value of the Preoperative Visit that shows that the time an anesthesiologist spends visiting with and speaking to patients prior to operation correlates directly to calming and even diminishing nervousness more than using medication like Versed, a cousin of Valium." Taking the time to connect and align themselves with the people they serve elevates doctors, and all professionals, really, to a much higher level of respect, trust, and authority.

Another form of authoritative alignment is reflected in your ability to match up what you want to say with how you say it. "I'd really like to have that report on my desk next week, okay?" will not get people hopping the same way as a definitive, "Please turn in that report next Tuesday at the latest." Rudeness is never okay, but dancing around what you want and trying to appease people will never earn you the respect you desire.

DETACHMENT

Authority exists in the fine line between letting people know they matter and that you care, and also in being confident enough to stand back and let people make up their minds about you or what you're saying without more input from you. Peter Bregman, who consults and advises CEOs and their top management teams on leadership and workplace issues, says, "It can't matter to you too much whether someone follows your advice. If you're needy, that reads as a *lack* of authority. But to say, 'I've actually thought a lot about this and I can share my opinion and perspective, and then *you* make a choice'— that reads as real authority. Even though it's counterintuitive, I always avoid *convincing* people of things. I'm more interested in offering people value when they're ready to hear it." He is describing authoritative detachment, and Maria the cobbler was a master at it. She'd state your problem and how to solve it, then step back to let you make the final decision. Her authority was in the absolute confidence she exuded that should you reject her advice or go to a different business, you'd be sorry, because she was the best. She wanted to work with you; she didn't *need* to work with you. Had Al Gore managed a greater sense of detachment during his presidential run, had his mind-set been more "I'd be a great president but I can't control what people think, so I'm going to offer my best and let the chips fall where they may," he would have shown greater authority during his debates, and maybe he'd have won. Think about it—when discussing politics with someone with different views than you, have you ever been convinced to see their perspective when they hammer at you nonstop about why you're wrong, and not only are you wrong, your wrongness is tearing the country down? Of course not. But if you've ever been lucky enough to have a productive, interesting political conversation with someone who feels differently about some issues than you do, any common ground was likely found because you were both willing to step back and listen. You didn't argue as though the stakes were dire; you gave each other room to work through your ideas, ask questions, and really hear where the other person was coming from without simultaneously planning what you were going to say next. Detachment keeps you from looking desperate, an excellent authoritative quality that plays well whether you're interviewing for a job, negotiating contracts, or pitching new clients.

AUTHORITY **CHEAT SHEET**

AUTHORITATIVE VOICE

▶ *Pitch: Resonance, inflection, audible punctuation*

▶ *Pace: Crisp, short, succinct, and declarative sentences (just say it, already!); Variety—mix it up to keep your listener engaged*

▶ *Volume: Audibly clear and strong, confident, power behind your words*

AUTHORITATIVE BODY LANGUAGE

▶ *Hold your chin up*

▶ *Walk with a confident gait*

▶ *Hold a strong posture*

▶ *Keep your hands above the waist*

▶ *Make eye contact while speaking and listening (in cultures where direct eye contact is acceptable)*

▶ *Wear a wardrobe that matches your personality yet is appropriate for the situation and culture*

AUTHORITATIVE PRESENCE

▶ *Work on your inner confidence*

▶ *Stay true to your inner conviction*

▶ *Encourage others*

▶ *Be authentic*

▶ *Be respectful*

▶ *Remain measured and unflappable*

CHAPTER 5 | **TURN UP YOUR AUTHORITY**

EXTERNAL ASSESSMENT

Train Your Eyes

Pay attention to how people hold themselves, how they use their body to convey their message, and how their nonverbal communication affects and influences you. Within professional settings, your social circle, and out on the street, watch for how people communicate and convey an air of authority through their physical presentation. Chances are you'll become aware of their authority before they recognize it in themselves.

Turn Up Your Ears

Within professional settings, your social circle, and out on the street, listen for vocal variety of PPV—pitch, pace, and volume. When developing AWE-wareness of authority in voice, listen for how others communicate command, confidence, and conviction with their voice. Who sounds authoritative?

NOTICE PITCH. Do those around you speak with an artificially high-pitched, nasal, or singsongy voice? Or do you hear true resonance? A strength behind their words? Do they sound authentic, as if they're using their "real" voice?

NOTICE PACE. People who talk too slow or at a monotonous pace are often perceived as distinctly lacking authority. You don't want to sound the same at every turn. A varied pace combined with inflection creates suspense and drama and keeps your listener interested and engaged. Predictable equals boring. And boring lacks authority.

NOTICE VOLUME. Remember, the loudest guy in the room is often the weakest guy in the room. One can still speak in understated and low tones and communicate authority, and by picking the right time to interject one's message. Authority can be audibly delivered in a very measured way. Don't just listen for the loudest guy in the room; rather become more aware of the *variations* of audible authority. Listen for how all types of voices come across to others and how, specifically, different voices affect and influence you.

NOTICE ATTITUDE. Communicating conviction is a good thing. It generates respect and draws attention. On the other hand, mansplaining or communicating an overconfidence that patronizes your audience will most definitely turn them away. As will cutting people off midsentence to bring it "BTM"—back to me.

SELF-ASSESSMENT

Once you get to the point where you can turn the observations you are making of other people on yourself, it's time to turn your critical eye inward. Take a moment to listen to the recordings you made before beginning this chapter.

Assess Your Voice

Ask yourself, or rather, listen to yourself: Does my voice have command? Do I speak up and make myself heard? Does the delivery of my words convey a strong conviction and a belief in what I'm saying? Do *I believe* my own arguments and is my confidence audibly coming through? Voices with authority generally sound purposeful, declarative, and strong. And remember—strong isn't a synonym for loud. One can deliver a powerful message in measured and understated tones, and by picking just the right time to speak up. Conversely, voices that are monotone, mumbling, and lacking articulation are perceived as weak and *un*-authoritative. Artificially high-pitched and singsongy voices also lack conviction, in large part because they sound fake or forced. Hemming and hawing, using filler words ("ah," "um," and "like"), or speaking cryptically can also introduce a level of doubt in your message and a lack of confidence in yourself. Both undermine your authority.

Refer back to the Cheat Sheet on page 73 for a full description of authority in voice. Ask for feedback: Do I deliver audible authority? Is there conviction behind my words? Do *I* sound as if I believe in what I'm saying? Do I speak as if I deserve to be heard? When I choose to, do my words command the room?

Fill in the blank: Today, I describe my voice as _____. On a scale of 1–5, I rate the level of authority in my voice at _____. Record and rank yourself every day to build self-awareness and become cognizant of variations in how you communicate and what you need to do to improve.

Assess Your Body Language

Ask yourself, and look at yourself: Does my stance convey a sense of authority, along with a belief in my message and myself? Upright posture, direct eye contact, and a commanding gait exhibit an air of authority. Confident hand gestures and facial expressions also communicate authority, as does a general sense of comfort in your own skin.

Assess Your Dress

Ask yourself, and look at yourself: Do my clothes communicate that I'm an authority in my chosen field? Do I present myself appropriately for my setting and my audience? Being a talent agent is a big personality job that fits me well, and yet I've learned that I deliver my message much more effectively when I dial down my wardrobe. If I were to wear loud suits, coupled with my higher-volume personality, I'd likely overwhelm my audience and not only risk losing their attention, but also undermine my authority. If you're a big personality, you also may consider dialing down the "big." Conversely, if you tend to be more reserved, you may want to dress bolder so as not to fade into the scenery. That said, don't stray too far away from your essence. (For me this means no ties. I've never felt confident wearing one and I resist putting one on. In fact, my aversion is so strong that my wife agreed to include on our wedding invitation: "Ties discouraged.") Authenticity in dress and presenting yourself in a real and relatable way boosts your audience's perception of your authority. So ask yourself: Is my outward presentation authentically me? Or am I playing a role?

Refer back to the Cheat Sheet on page 73 for a full description of authority in body language. Ask for feedback: Do I carry and present myself with an air of authority? Is my body language strong? Does my overall "look" convey a sense of authority? Do I dress appropriately for my chosen field? Is there conviction behind my words? Do *I* sound as if I believe in what I'm saying? Do I speak as if I deserve to be heard? When I choose to, do my words command the room?

Fill in the blank: Today, I describe my body language as _____. On a scale of 1–5, I rate the level of authority in my body language and wardrobe choices at _____.

Over time you'll be able to judge when it's important to be either more or less authoritative and when to modify your "look" as you become more adept at both reading yourself and reading how others read you.

Assess Your Presence

Does your general presence communicate inner confidence, authenticity, and a sense of alignment with your audience? Refer back to the Cheat Sheet on page 73 for a full description. And then assess how people are *reacting* to you. Ask yourself:

Do people look up when I enter a room?

When I speak, do people listen?

Do I generally feel heard?

Do people take me seriously?

Do I often take a leadership position?

Do people ask for my opinion and tend to follow my advice?

Do I generally feel respected?

Do I respect others?

Or,

Do my words tend to fall on deaf ears?

Do people tend to tune me out before I make my point?

Do I often feel like I'm losing people when I speak?

Do my words tend to get lost in translation?

Do people interrupt and talk over me?

Do people often dismiss or ignore my advice?

Do I go relatively unnoticed in a room?

Do I get passed up for projects or promotions I'm technically qualified to do?

If you answered yes to any of the last eight questions, you may benefit greatly from improving your impression of authority. Consider what specifically you could do to improve it. Changes to your voice? Body language? Wardrobe? General presence?

Rehearse Loud and Proud

The most effective way to develop more confidence and authority is through repetitive practice. Pull copy from a variety of printed sources—newspapers, magazines, books—even mail. In fact, the more tedious and stale the copy, the better. Your challenge is to breathe certainty into every word. Read out loud and record yourself. Practice speaking in front of a mirror. (Most of us don't know what our face is doing when we're speaking.) Does it look as if you believe what you're reading? Better yet, does it sound as if you believe what you're *saying*? Continue this practice at home and when you feel ready, practice with your spouse, a friend, your Uber driver. There are many opportunities within a day to infuse a higher level of conviction into your words. With practice and repetition, you will sound and look like the pinnacle of professionalism and skill you already know you are.

MORE TIPS:

- Build your confidence. When we're afraid, nervous, or insecure, our breath tends to come in quicker, shallower bursts, making it difficult to support our voice. Many of our bad vocal habits, from speaking too high to speaking too fast, are due to nerves. When you're confident in your abilities and your right to belong, you speak more measuredly. If sounding more confident means practicing what you want to say before you go into your boss's office to ask for a raise, so be it.

  Beth Mowins points out that women are in a double bind when it comes to being authoritative. On one hand, if they speak too softly or high, they aren't seen as leadership material. On the other hand, especially in male-dominated fields, women who assert themselves are often chided for sounding "too authoritative." It's enraging and unfair that women have to walk this line. "Whether it's consciously or subconsciously, that is in the back of your mind. You don't want to be *too* strong but you do have to pick and choose your moments where you stand your ground and fight for your space."

  Mowins says she has found that establishing her authority has gotten easier, however, now that she's often the most experienced person on the crew. Her depth of knowledge, along with her confidence, commands attention and respect. Her advice for young women, and especially those hoping to break into her field, is to "earn the right to be there. You can't control how other people see you, but you can control how you see yourself and how you present yourself and how you promote yourself."

- To lower your pitch, concentrate on supporting your voice with your breath. When speaking, try to use your belly muscles to breathe, expanding on the inhale and tightening on the exhale. This will help you lower your pitch to sound more authoritative, but you'll also find in the next chapter of this book that it's the foundation for building warmth into your voice as well. The two are not mutually exclusive, as you'll discover.

- Work on your resonance, also known as timbre. This refers to the quality that gives some texture to your voice, and how it sounds is determined by whether the air primarily comes out of your mouth, your pharynx, or your nose. If you speak mostly from your nose, you'll sound like Nathan Lane. I adore Nathan Lane, but I don't want you to sound like him. Nor do you want to sound like Henry Kissinger, who sounds like his vocal cords are so tight the air can't get out. Try to channel your inner James Earl Jones instead (without artificially lowering your voice; you're trying to optimize your voice, not disguise it). Relax your throat and let your breath come out of your mouth.
- Sometimes we speak in a higher voice to sound more ingratiating or less threatening. People who command authority don't worry about that. Own your ideas and opinions.
- If you make a statement, make a statement. Adding a question mark to the end of every sentence, a habit known as upspeak, communicates doubt in yourself and your material.
- Pay attention to the feeling in your throat, jaw, neck, and shoulders. When we tense up, our breathing shifts and we can't support our voice. If anything starts to feel strained, take a breath and relax.
- Slow down. Don't mumble; vary your delivery. Do you notice people moving slightly away, or do you get the side-eye from people nearby? Lower your volume. See people leaning in to hear you? Speak up.
- Pay attention to your stance and gait. Do those around you stand tall or shrink? Does their posture communicate that they are comfortable in their own skin? George W. Bush walked like a cowboy with his shoulders back.

- Keep your hands above the waist and use gestures judiciously. Don't cover your mouth with your hands when speaking.

- Assuming you're working in an environment and culture where direct eye contact is acceptable, work on keeping eye contact with others while speaking and listening to others. That means put down your phone! That goes for when you're at home, too (something my wife and children would tell you I need to work on).

CHAPTER 6 | # WARMTH:
THE SEED OF TRUST

In the first year of IF Management's life, when I was a relatively new agent trying to build my credibility, and clientele, I had the opportunity to interview with a smart young newscaster looking for representation. I welcomed her into my office and introduced her to my colleague. Then we started talking about her career aspirations and what I could do for her. I thought she had extraordinary potential and talent and I was eager to work with her. I turned on my charm, told my most interesting stories, and by the end of our conversation, I was confident that we'd hit it off and that she not only was impressed with what I could offer, but also sensed that I was someone she could trust. I was sure she'd sign with us. But as soon as she left the office, my colleague turned to me and said, "We will never hear from that woman again."

What was he talking about? She loved us!

His words stung. Still, I appreciated the honest feedback. It was, after all, what I had sworn to give my clients and employees. If I wanted to dish it out, I had to be able to take it.

"Why?" I challenged him.

"All you did was talk. You didn't connect."

I was dumbfounded. Was this true? I replayed the scene in my mind, this time muting my brilliant repartee and dazzling salesmanship and focusing on the actual conversation that had happened.

Shit. He was right.

The problem wasn't only that I didn't listen. I sincerely wanted to do my best by this person, and I did encourage her to tell me her aspirations and goals. But once I knew what they were, I had bulldozed my way through the interview in an attempt to clear away any possible objection she could find to signing with me. For example, if she said, "I'm interested in getting on CNN," my reply probably went something like this:

"You want CNN? I know exactly what we're going to do. Listen to me. We're going to put a tape together with all your clips. I'm going to show them how smart you are, and how much you know about world affairs and politics. And then I'm going to call the head of CNN. He's a friend of mine. . . ." But at thirty years old, her best asset was her law degree. I was so busy puffing myself up to sound important and influential, I didn't stop to think if giving her what she wanted was the right move. What I should have told her was that while she'd been on the air a couple of times, that didn't give her the chops to be a CNN correspondent. It was something she could aspire to in a few years with more experience. At this stage in the game, with her law background, we should have aimed for something like Court TV. I was listening to her, but only to the degree that I was waiting for her to give me another opportunity to prove my skills and knowledge. Knowing that she was a hot commodity and was interviewing with competitors, including a former colleague of mine, I felt compelled to prove how smart I was. This time, however, my horrible habit of interrupting, talking over people, and generally blabbing on had finally caught up to me and bitten me squarely in the butt.

As my colleague predicted, we never did hear from this young newscaster again. She signed with another agency and soon after, she did in fact wind up on Court TV, which was a burgeoning and hot cable network on the heels of the O. J. Simpson trial.

I was happy to see this young woman succeed, and grateful that she had given me a chance to learn my lesson early. After that botched interview, I made a resolution to stop talking so much in meetings and let the other participants, whether potential clients, current clients, or employees, have their say. It paid off. Only eight months later, I was able to hire a second full-time employee and I moved into a bigger, nicer office in a better neighborhood. It was May 1997, and my two employees were two guys just out of college, named Lowell Taub and Jared Horowitz. Today Lowell is the senior VP of all talent marketing for CAA sports, and Jared is the vice chairman of Newmark Knight Frank Realty, and we are still good friends. The understanding and professional respect we showed each other was a tremendous component of our relationship and the relationships we built with our clients and, I believe, a big part of why the business grew so fast.

MISTAKE POSTMORTEM

The problem wasn't only that I was rude to turn what was supposed to be a conversation about her into a monologue about me. This kind of redirection had worked before, such as when I was a young kid fighting to be heard at a dinner table surrounded by three opinionated siblings, and even more recently with other clients who were less in demand and had fewer options with regards to signing with an agency. I was at a point in my career where I still hadn't built a strong reputation and had a lot to prove; I had to talk about myself and what I had to offer.

The problem definitely wasn't that I didn't care, either. I cared so much I became needy, thus undermining my authority exactly as Peter Bregman described two chapters ago. I hadn't yet developed enough confidence to practice the art of authoritative detachment, which allows people in the room to evaluate you, your product, or your services on their merits and make up their own minds.

The problem was that I was more concerned about projecting authority than warmth, and one simply doesn't have the same impact without the other. If I had to guess, the young newscaster probably believed everything I told her we could do for her—I had enough experience in the industry to establish my authority and I knew what I was talking about. But she didn't trust me. I hadn't bothered to build a connection, to help her see our commonality. I didn't layer my authority with warmth.

WHY WARMTH MATTERS

Warmth is perhaps the most underappreciated tool in the AWE-some toolkit. In her brilliantly funny book, *Maybe You Should Talk to Someone*, psychotherapist Lori Gottlieb recounts counseling a couple in which the wife turned to her husband and said, "'You know what three words would be more romantic than *I love you?*' 'You look beautiful?' he tried. 'No,' his wife said, 'I understand you.'" That's the essence of warmth—the sense of connection that springs from being understood and making the effort to understand. It's not just a crucial factor in romantic love; it's imperative in all successful relationships. It's where trust comes from, and its absence or presence can have tremendous implications across all areas of life. For example, a 2017 study by the Centers for Disease Control and Prevention (CDC) reported that while the difference in life expectancy between white men and black men in the United States has shrunk significantly, black mortality rates still lag by about 3.5 years compared to the mortality rates of white men until they reach the age of sixty-five, after which they actually outlive white men (the lead author of the study, Tim Cunningham, surmised that by that age, many men suffering from the chronic diseases and unhealthy behaviors that frequently kill black men—often a consequence of higher levels of poverty and lower levels of education compared to whites—have already died). Closing that gap would require improving the rate at which black men pursue preventative care, a rate that saw a sharp drop starting in 1972, when it was revealed that for the last forty years researchers at Tuskegee University in Alabama had been lying to participants of a federally funded medical study, all poor black men. Told they were getting free health care for "bad blood," in fact they were recruited so researchers could study the effects of untreated syphilis. The participants were withheld treatment for the disease even after it was discovered in 1947 that penicillin could cure it, leading many men to unnecessarily suffer and die. Understandably, the scandal caused many black men to adopt a deep mistrust of the medical system, making them reluctant to visit doctors or seek preventative care. In 2018, researchers at Stanford and the University of California, Berkeley, wanted to find out what could persuade black men to get more preventative care services. They invited black men to visit a clinic for free preventative health screening. The participants who attended, mostly poor and without primary care doctors, were shown a photo of their randomly chosen doctor and given a chance to choose from five services. Then they met their doctors in person. In the end, the number of preventative services the men originally selected, regardless of the color of their assigned doctor, was about the same. The number of services the men selected and received *after* they met with their doctors greatly differed. Men who met with a black doctor were 56 percent more likely to get flu shots, 47 percent more likely to get screened for diabetes, and 72 percent more likely to get cholesterol screenings. Again, the men consistently elected the same number of preventative services before meeting with their doctors in person, even though they knew the doctor's race ahead of time. It was only after meeting with the doctor in person that the number of preventative services they were willing to do, especially services that might involve a blood draw or a shot, changed. And the men who were *most* distrustful of the medical system before coming in were also the most willing to change their minds and agree to more preventative services after meeting with a black doctor. Why?

According to Owen Garrick, one of the coauthors of the study, the difference lay in the connection the black doctors were able to establish with their black patients. "We found that the black doctors actually wrote more notes compared to the nonblack doctors about their patients, and often those notes talked about their non-health care issues—a wedding is coming up, will the Warriors repeat as NBA champions? Like, so nonmedical issues."

The black doctors were able to overcome *decades* of skepticism and mistrust not only by establishing their authority, but by taking an intense personal interest in their patients and finding commonalities. There are other possible explanations for the results—maybe the black doctors were better, maybe there was discrimination—but given that the patients showed no preference for white or black doctors on feedback forms delivered after the experiment, there's no indication that the nonblack doctors were biased or racist, nor reason to doubt these doctors' bedside manner or good intent. The evidence strongly suggests that it was the type of communication that made the difference. A communication that built trust. In my world, I label that type of communication "Warmth." In this particular study, that trust grew between two people who might have shared cultural, ethnic, or religious kinship. But the power of warmth is that it can allow you to create that bond and trust with anyone, no matter how different from you they may seem. When we want to look for commonalities, we find them. One would hope that after seeing these results, the nonblack doctors would recognize that they have to work harder to create commonalities with patients of a different race, acknowledging that their patients' background, cultural history, and experience of the world may be vastly different from their own. Difference is not an unsurmountable obstacle (it's also not always visible or obvious). It may just require you to work a little harder and a little smarter. So the entire exercise of building warmth is about teaching ourselves to always look for those commonalities through your day-to-day life with everyone you encounter. How? Through humility, engagement, relatability, attentiveness, and vulnerability. Some of these qualities are expressed through output—what you're putting out into the world—and some through input—what you invite and allow other people to express. Those who balance the two successfully are AWEsome leaders.

WARM OUTPUT

We've already discussed the best ways to express authority and communicate with others. But managers and leaders who deliver authority without warmth often tend to devolve into authoritarianism, expecting high performance of employees or teams for no other reason than it has been demanded of them. Effective leaders are authoritative, not authoritarian. The difference is profound. With the latter, teams perform their best out of fear of punishment; in the former, people perform their best out of a desire to contribute to the success of something they care about, whether it's an individual project or task or an entire company mission. Which leadership style do you think encourages the most creative, innovative, energetic, determined thinking and problem solving? Which will elicit a strong sense of duty and commitment, the kind that sustains teams even when the stakes and expectations are high and the road gets rough? You get that kind of performance and dedication by delivering authority with warm output that conveys authenticity, humility, empathy, and vulnerability. It's indicative of our culture that many of my clients balk when I suggest they be more vulnerable and warm in the workplace. Won't that undermine their authority? It will not. Presenting yourself with vulnerability is not about showing weakness or being too soft. It's also not about TMI or exposing all the sensitive details of your personal life. In fact, that's where people get it wrong—when they feel pressured to share more than feels comfortable and wind up feeling like they're playing a role to get ahead at the workplace, they're not being authentic and true to themselves and *that* undermines authority. Similarly, the second people suspect that you're oversharing to gain favor or pity, or to create an artificial bond, you've lost them. It also matters what kind of vulnerability you reveal. Even psychologist and bestselling author Brené Brown, one of the chief promoters of vulnerability as a leadership tool, cautions, "You don't stand in front of people who work for you and say, 'I don't know what I'm doing and it's all going to hell.'" By her definition, vulnerability and courage are the same thing. Or as she said in a TED Talk, "Vulnerability is the birthplace of innovation, creativity, and change."

Vulnerability in the workplace is simply about revealing that you're human, which makes you relatable to everyone in the room. Showing the right amount of vulnerability actually boosts your authority, so long as it's done selectively, judiciously, and authentically.

Tom Coughlin, former coach, now executive VP of football operations for the Jacksonville Jaguars, learned this the hard way.

Shortly after joining the New York Giants in 2004, the coach became so famous for his sternness and rigidity he had his own time zone—Coughlin Standard Time—which every die-hard football fan knows to mean you're only on time if you arrive five minutes early. When I spoke to Coughlin for this book, I arrived five minutes early. He was punctual, of course. That's about the only thing that hasn't changed about him since he nearly lost his coaching job with the Giants more than a decade ago.

By his own admission, the silver-haired coach in the wire-rimmed glasses taught a "tough brand of football where you work long and you work hard. You make it as tough as you can possibly make it and those that remain, as they say, will be champions. That's what I firmly believed. That's the way I approached it. There's no warm and fuzzy. You don't go in and be soft." It was an approach that had worked for him. Coughlin had lots of authority and energy that had allowed him to take the Jacksonville Jaguars to the playoffs and the AFC championship game. Yet in his first three seasons with the Giants, Coughlin failed to win even *one* playoff game, and as the team headed into the 2007 season on the heels of a disappointing 8–8 record, the Giants' highest-profile star running back, Tiki Barber, retired at the top of this career, with no love lost between himself and his boss. Players complained that he was obsessed with minutiae like the color of the players' socks on and off the field (dress socks only in hotel lobbies, white socks only on the field, or pay a fine) but not the stuff that really mattered. One anonymous player publicly called Coughlin out for running the team like a dictatorship.

Asked about this characterization of Coughlin, Barber told me, "He was never very good at communicating his task. It was just, 'Do as I say,' and we didn't like that. I don't think anybody liked that." No, they didn't. Hall of Fame defensive end Michael Strahan told a reporter that several members of the team had come to him for advice on how to deal with Coughlin. "We hated him. And it was real. It was no public persona. We hated the man." Another anonymous teammate said, "He's not the type of coach we're going to go and put everything on the line for. Guys don't play for him; they play because they have to play and you're not going to win that way."

Sure enough, the team had "free fallen," and Coughlin's bark and brusque ways had worn everybody out. He "spent more time worrying about whether his players were wearing appropriate dress socks in hotel lobbies than he did about connecting with them as human beings." And it wasn't only the players demanding change, but also the fans and the media. So long as his team was winning, his behavior behind the scenes and on the sidelines didn't matter to the public, but once they started losing, they started to turn on him. During the second half of a game against the New Orleans Saints, the crowd started chanting, "Fire Coughlin."

"How can you look at the production of Sunday and not think that, O.K., there's some issue here?" Coughlin said at the time.

After mulling over whether to fire Coughlin, team co-owner John Mara invited his coach back but advised him to "take something off his fastball" with regard to how he treated his players. Coughlin remembers, "What they were all saying was, 'He never shows us that he really cares about us.'" At the same time, he was confronted by his own family in an old-fashioned intervention and told by his son "Dad, these people hate you. They're all writing terrible things about you." They knew he was on thin ice.

That's when Coughlin took the gloves off and did something he'd never done before—he met with print media and television reporters one-on-one and asked them point-blank, "Tell me what you don't like about me."

"And what I came away with was that they wanted more from *me*. I came to the realization—I can do better. They deserve to have more respect from me. They deserve my attention. I can do a better job of communicating with them. You can call it humility. You can call it whatever you want, but that's basically what it was."

You know what I call it, of course. It's warmth.

Anyone who followed the 2007 football season likely remembers a major transformation as Coughlin began to address the media with less curtness and a more open attitude. Stories started coming out about the strange behavior he was exhibiting with his players. Coughlin says, "Charles Way, who was my player development guy, said to me, 'Coach, let them see you like you are with your grandkids.' So, practice would be over and I'd be rolling in the grass with my grandkids, throwing the ball around." The only thing more shocking might have been the day Coughlin canceled practice and took the team bowling. "It was fun, and a way of letting players see you in a caring manner, and letting them know you are human and passionate and concerned about them outside of football. . . . And because we communicated so well and believed in each other and loved each other, that manifested itself on the field in so many games that we won late with mental toughness and staying together."

"The issue was never that Tom was a bad guy," recalls Tiki Barber. "I think that was the biggest issue I had with him. I couldn't reconcile how he treated us versus how I knew he actually was."

In addition to showing himself to his players in a warmer light, Coughlin created a leadership council composed of players from each position. "Like a board of directors," he explained, who would deliver the team message and important strategies back to the players.

"It was a huge change," admits Coughlin, "but I wanted the players' buy-in, and the way to do that was to make them feel like it was *their* team and they had a say."

Eventually, Coughlin's efforts started to pay off. "They did begin to understand that I cared about them," said Coughlin. "I've always believed completely in 'team' and acknowledging the fact that you can't do it without the other person, and you understand the part that they play in the puzzle. It takes everybody. You can't win alone."

Coughlin's public image really started to improve when the team started winning. He took his team all the way to Glendale, Arizona, and a stunning 17–14 Super Bowl win over the previously undefeated and twelve-point favorite New England Patriots in the biggest Super Bowl upset since Joe Namath's New York Jets in 1969. He then took the Giants to another Super Bowl win in 2011 and will eventually be enshrined to the same pantheon as legendary two-time Super Bowl–winning coaches Vince Lombardi and Don Shula in the Pro Football Hall of Fame.

It begs the question: did the Giants become a winning team as a result of Coughlin warming up? Well, Coughlin had a good team, and then he had a champion team—with the exact same players. People simply perform better when they feel supported. A sales manager who berates her team for not making quota isn't doing anything to help her team make quota. She's probably making it harder. Teams that work together and know they've all got each other's backs tend to draw the best out of their individual players, no matter what their field. When I first got into business, a mentor told me, "Your employees aren't your friends. Better they should fear you than love you." I didn't get it, and I never ran my company that way. If you've hired the right people or have established the right environment, people won't need to feel threatened or intimidated; they'll be internally motivated to succeed.

The team succeeded because the players felt respected and heard, and they were able to give their own input to a coach who was willing to listen.

People who feel cared for and respected work harder. It's just a fact. Retired United States Navy admiral and former chairman of the Joint Chiefs of Staff Mike Mullen agrees. The highly decorated veteran, who built his life and career on service, retired in 2011 after forty-three years as one of only three men appointed to four different four-star assignments in the navy's history. By virtue of his high rank in one of the most hierarchical institutions in America, it would be easy to assume that he would not have seen any need to "connect" with those who served under him. Yet throughout his career, Admiral Mullen made a point of infusing his delivery and message with great warmth. He sees it as crucial to developing good soldiers.

"I've had to overcome this stereotypical view of an admiral or a general because that's what gets carried into the room," he revealed. "If I reinforce the stereotype rather than break it down, or reinforce my level of authority, then that closes down a conversation pretty quickly. And not just the conversation, but the totality of my approach—my ability to interact, mentor and impact soldiers' careers. . . . That's my challenge—I'm a very senior guy and I've got an hour at an FOB [forward operating base] in Afghanistan with, you know, 30 soldiers who consider themselves on the 9th ring of hell, I gotta get them to open up pretty quickly. What I want to do is have a conversation. And the way I do that is to first get their whole chain of command out of the room and then I get personal with them. And fast. Where are you from? Who's your favorite football team? Why does Dallas suck? I ask this because, you know, I'm a Skins guy."

Admiral Mullen says that he reveals his "human side" to shift the energy in the room. He also relies on humor, a communication tool that often surprises his military audience.

"I'm lousy at telling a joke but I'm pretty good on my feet in terms of injecting humor as I go. And what humor does for me, whether it's a very small or big audience, is that it engages people. It just lets the guard down and puts the individual I'm speaking with at ease. I use sports and humor a lot, and I can almost always get a conversation started. And then I get to the more serious stuff, where I extract from them, if you will, what concerns they have and how I can help them."

I asked Admiral Mullen about this delicate balancing act where he has to maintain authority through voice, body language, and presence, and also communicate a level of relatability to get his subordinates to open up to him.

"This is my challenge as a very senior guy. What I've learned over time is that what's most important is not what I say but my *interaction* with my audience."

Far from undermining your authority, allowing people to see your humanity deepens your connections, inspiring greater loyalty. Again, being warm doesn't necessarily have to be about revealing yourself or urging others to reveal. It's simply about communicating with honesty and authenticity. It's about being real. As long as you've got your technical proficiency and knowledge—the 15 percent—totally covered, it cannot hurt you.

ESPN college football sideline reporter Holly Rowe was already one of the most beloved in her field by viewers, coaches, and athletes, but when she went public in 2017 with her cancer diagnosis, her fans rallied around her even more. Rowe worked through her rigorous treatment plan, and often spoke candidly on camera about the highs and lows of her recovery process. Viewers watched her show up on the sidelines, and not as a superhero or with a game face, but as an imperfect human being whom we could all relate to and root for. ESPN senior coordinating producer Lee Fitting told the Associated Press, "Holly's energy and year-long dedication to ESPN is a testament to her strength and resiliency all while courageously battling cancer."

Did you catch that? The network perceived Holly's vulnerability as a *strength*, and one of her *greatest assets*. In the midst of treatment, ESPN renewed Holly's contract *and* extended her deal.

Maybe you're still not convinced that sharing much about your personal life is a good idea at work. What else can you do? The same thing you did when you wanted to communicate authority, through PPV (pitch, pace, and volume) and body language. People won't listen to you, trust you, or believe you if they don't inherently feel a connection to you. Think about it: if someone lacks warmth, you don't warm up to them. When someone gives you the sense that they're closed off, either through their words, body language, or facial expression, you're less inclined to open up to them. Or do business with or have a relationship with them.

PPV

Think of each conversation you have as a collection of little sound bites. There will be moments when you need to speak with lots of authority, but if you don't modulate it with warmth, you'll lose your audience. How do we do it in a way that doesn't undermine our authority? We've already established that a high pitch, a speedy pace, and a blaring volume hurt your authority. They hurt your ability to express warmth, too. This can be crucial to getting what you want out of a negotiation or in problem solving. If you're running roughshod over a conversation, you're likely not paying close enough attention to reading people, and therefore not attuned to what they need. Steven Shapiro, a partner at the Wall Street firm GoldenTree Capital, says that whenever he's in a negotiation and things start getting a little contentious, or he has a disagreement with a business partner, he makes a pointed effort to take a breath and calmly say, "Tell me what you're worried about." By actively keeping his pitch and volume steady, and slowing the pace of the conversation, he deescalates the tension and makes sure the other side knows he is willing to listen. Ceding the "floor" for a few minutes boosts his warmth—thus helping his opposition feel less on the defensive—without undermining his authority. Eighty percent of the time, he says, he discovers that they're assuming something about his motives or plans, or projecting concerns about things that hadn't even crossed his mind. Once that misperception is cleared up, the conversation usually resumes in a much more productive way for both sides.

Body Language

Nonverbal signals communicate volumes. Arms tightly folded across your chest, lack of eye contact, the absence of a smile, or a generally cool vibe can and most often will doom your message and sabotage the overall impression you make. There are plenty of people in the public space who have shown us how expressions of warmth can translate directly to strong likability. My favorite is Al Roker, host and weatherman of NBC's *Today* show and who embodies nearly every variable of physical warmth. His tone is engaging; his body language is open and relaxed. He smiles easily and looks people in the eye. When Al was in the early stages of starting his production company, we briefly shared office space in the legendary Fisk building in midtown Manhattan. Al was already a household name, a celebrity in his own right. Still, whenever we crossed paths, Al made me feel like *I* was the star, and from what I've observed, Al treats everyone this way. Most people who meet Al feel like they've met a friend because he's right there with you. His warmth comes through and because of this, you warm *to him*.

Dr. Michael Levine, a urological surgeon with Integrated Medical Professionals, PLLC, is in a teaching advisory role to residents at Northwell Health, where he routinely gives instruction on surgical technique and also invites residents to scrub in and accompany him on patient rounds. He acknowledges that teaching young doctors how to interact is now imperative to helping them succeed in the field.

"I came from an era where people didn't contradict the doctor," says Levine. "They didn't challenge the doctor. They humbly accepted their advice. Now, patients want more. They want a conversation. They want a connection. They're not just interested in what you have to say professionally; they want to feel embraced and convinced that your recommendations are sound. Which means doctors now need to deliver, not just their expertise, but also an overall experience. You can have all the expertise in the world but if you don't deliver the *right* kind of experience, you're not accepted."

Some of the tips he offers his residents:

- Don't speak to your patient with your hand on the doorknob, it makes people feel like you're in a hurry to get away and your mind is already focused elsewhere.
- Point your toes in the direction of your patient to make them feel that you're completely engaged, and not just there to dispense good medical advice.
- Take your time and convince them that you've given them the time to answer all their questions.

  This would be good advice no matter what field you're in. I might add:

- Smile often.
- Keep your gaze soft.
- Make eye contact but don't stare.
- Keep your face relaxed. If you feel your eyebrows knitting together or your lips tightening, take a breath and see if that helps.
- Lean forward. This helps you stay engaged and conveys your interest to others. Don't do it the whole time you're speaking with someone, lest you make people feel crowded.

Warmth is tangible. You *feel* it and it feels good. The warmest person I know (bias alert) is my wife, Raquel. She communicates her generosity through both her words and physical expression. As an example, her first instinct when meeting someone is to hug them in a full embrace. She's the one who pointed out one of my weaknesses: I used to give what she calls "ass-out" hugs. "You'd go in for an embrace but not fully commit. Your arms would be around me, but the rest of your body was sticking out somewhere behind you." Whether hugs would be appropriate in your workplace is a matter of culture and judgment. We're big on hugs in my office, but yours may not be, and it's your responsibility to be perceptive enough to recognize when the gesture would be welcome and appreciated, and when you need to stick to a handshake (practice AWE strategies and your self-awareness will improve so much, this shouldn't be difficult). Don't ever impose a hug on someone who might not want one, and when in doubt, play things safe and skip it. But the bigger point Raquel makes isn't about the hug, it's about my commitment, or lack thereof, to it. "If you're going to engage with someone, fully engage. Whether it's with a hug or speaking to someone across a table, use your physical expressions to show that you're focused on them." In other words, if you decide to give or accept a hug, don't do it half-assed.

We're all likely to have people in our private lives who know us well and can gently teach us a thing or two about how to turn up our own warmth. Like Coach Coughlin's family, and even some of his players, the people who love us see us at our best and want others to experience our best as well. Their advice and insight can be invaluable.

Connectability isn't only about warmly and authoritatively projecting your message *outward* into the world. People who are known for their warmth are also known for their willingness to listen, for their attentiveness, and for their ability to acknowledge people, whether it's a crowd or single individual. Perhaps counterintuitively, we also project a warm and authoritative message when we invite and accept input.

Input

Whatever business you're in, you are solving a problem. You can't do that if you don't make room for input using active, engaged listening to gain valuable information about what your audience most wants or needs. What is active listening? It's not just about being silent long enough to let someone else express themselves, but to do it without simultaneously planning a rebuttal or response. If you're actively listening, you're able to acknowledge the specificity of people's concerns or ideas, which by default would mean hearing them out until the end of their sentence or train of thought, not jumping in and interrupting as soon as you hear something you want to respond to. A lot of people have a hard time with the concept of acknowledgment, believing that it implies giving up the high ground on something they disagree with or agreeing to something they don't want to agree to. But that's not the case. To acknowledge is not to agree to anything;

it is simply to convey that you understand, whether you agree or not. Different from empathy, which can sometimes feel patronizing, acknowledgment is the act of making every effort to appreciate another person's perspective and anticipating what they need. Acknowledgment is crucial to understanding employees' and consumers' desires, and its absence can quickly lead to product mistakes and resentment. Deep listening, engaging, and acknowledging is a matter of letting the conversation breathe and addressing the micro issues raised as well as the macro topic, so that everyone feels completely heard.

Someone who is extraordinarily good at this is mild-mannered Canadian transplant Jeff Feig.

Imagine a Wall Street executive who oversaw a staff of more than four hundred in a dozen cities across three continents, and you probably wouldn't picture Jeff, a portly man with a propensity to sweat, who often walked into a room with his collar sticking up and food stains dotting his tie. Yet, in a decade at the helm of Citigroup's Global Foreign Exchange unit, this man—who did not hold the requisite MBA degree, who spoke with a lisp two decibels above a whisper, and who was once told by a new boss that he wasn't management material—doubled its revenue into a billion-and-a-half-dollar business. He also happened to have been one of the most beloved men at one of the world's largest banks, engendering so much love and loyalty along the way he was feted by the CEO when he announced his departure, and his former colleague Larry Evans said to me in a room filled with Feig's team: "Everyone in this room would eat glass for Jeff."

What propelled him to such great success? A unique brand of warmth.

"When I took over the business, it was definitely a cold place and people felt that they weren't looked after," recalls Feig. "I really tried to create an atmosphere where people felt like we cared about their development, cared about what they wanted, and wanted them to succeed." It was a tall order for a company this size, and Feig pulled it off by acknowledging people in a way that made them feel heard and let them believe that their voices mattered. "At Citi, I managed a team with four hundred people on average that were directly within my span of control, and with about twenty direct reports running different departments and divisions. And one of the things you learn working for a large company is that not every idea can be brought to fruition. Not every idea is good, and not everybody can get what they want, when they want it. So if someone came to me upset or disgruntled, I would always listen to their complaints. Let them say their piece. Not interrupt. I think listening is an underappreciated skill. Too many people want to talk. So I let *them* do most of the talking."

"Then once I understood the issue or the problem," Feig continued, "I'd try to present both sides in a balanced way [so that] I'm communicating that I'm concerned about them and the outcome, and I'm trying to help them analyze it. I would very often end my part of the conversation by saying, 'Does that make sense?' Not, did you hear me, but does that make sense to *you*?"

For the ten years Feig managed the Global Foreign Exchange unit by fostering a culture of acknowledgment, turnover was low, even during the tumultuous financial crisis of 2008, which battered Citigroup.

"While people in the business got very frustrated with a lot of things, especially when Citi almost had to shut its doors, and it was a pretty scary place at times—I was always honest. I never made promises I didn't think I could keep. I never told people things that weren't true. I think overall, the staff believed that their managers were looking out for them and their best interests. And people didn't want to leave that environment. If you look at the state of the business when I took over in '04, and when I left in '14, the turnover dropped dramatically, morale and satisfaction increased dramatically, and business did a lot better."

When I asked Feig what inspires his management style, he said simply, "Being a good manager is about treating people the way you would want to be treated. You just can't underestimate that in building a successful business."

In the tough Wall Street business, where looking the part is often synonymous with success and where physical diversions can undermine it, he smiles. "I definitely don't score high in presentation, but the one advantage is that it gets you noticed. I stand out."

I'd argue that what truly distinguishes Feig is his tremendous warmth. It's his biggest strength and what sets him apart from the rest.

WARM INCENTIVES

In every instance, there are long-term financial and professional benefits to infusing our interactions with warmth. To put it bluntly, being a better human is better for business. Costco's cofounder Jim Sinegal knew this. CEO until his retirement in 2012, Sinegal built Costco into one of the world's largest global retailers. He did it with a stringent attention to detail and quality, and by being ruthless about price, but he also insisted on creating a warm company culture, one that cared about the individual and tried to think ahead about what made people feel safe and loyal. By paying almost double its closest rival, Sam's Club, and offering generous benefits and job stability in the form of guaranteed hours, he successfully encouraged intense company loyalty, even admiration. His approach drew criticism from Wall Street, with one analyst grousing, "It's better to be an employee or a customer than a shareholder," or that he was "too benevolent," but Sinegal insisted, "Culture isn't the most important thing, it's the only thing. Culture drives every decision you make. Culture is everything." With a 12.9 percent annual growth rate, a turnover rate of just 7 percent compared to the usual 60–70 percent at other retailers, and almost nonexistent rates of employee theft (.11–.12 percent compared to the retail industry average of 1–2 percent), Sinegal proves that taking the warm approach—trying to see the world through someone else's eyes and wondering what would they need to be productive, happy, or satisfied—is good for business.

I've seen it work at my own company. I've been in business for twenty-three years, and five of my six employees, most of whom have been with me anywhere from ten to twenty years, have never worked anywhere else. They work hard, but I know they don't do it for me. They do it because they are committed to something we believe in that is bigger than all of us. And they also do it because they know that if the shit hits the fan, I will be there to help fix the problem. We have a tremendous sense of pride in our company, and I'd bank on any one of my employees. I'm extremely proud of the fact that I've developed so many good agents who don't feel like they have to move elsewhere in order to fulfill their professional potential. And it's not only possible because we're a small company. You can build warmth into a culture and management whether a company has forty or four thousand employees. It's just a mind-set.

Warmth builds loyalty and institutional knowledge. It communicates respect, and in doing so generates respect. What happens in these instances is the people working with you care more, about doing a good job, yes, but also about the bigger mission they work for. To that end, they want you to succeed. That translates into developing the trust we discussed at the beginning of this chapter, and a willingness to embrace risk and innovation, and also letting you know when mistakes have been made or when things aren't going the way they should long before they become crises, so you have time to fix problems or change direction. It means people care enough to tell you that problems exist before they metastasize. Whether you're running a football team, a hospital, a military unit, or an office division, if your colleagues or employees are afraid of you and don't feel comfortable talking to you, they'll let you sink.

Allowing for honest input requires humility. Interestingly, so does effective output. Some highly accomplished people, especially ones who have a strong sense of authority, struggle with this. But humility is actually tied to confidence. It's insecurity that causes people to talk too much. It's insecurity that makes it hard to listen to others. When you're confident in your knowledge and your expertise, you don't have to constantly remind people of your accomplishments or credentials. You don't have to insist that you are right. You're willing to listen to other people's thoughts or perspectives because you're not threatened by them. Once you learn to strike that perfect balance of input and output, you are free to be your authentic self. Best of all, you allow others to do the same.

If you're losing sales or struggling to form solid relationships, if you can't seem to make the right connections to get ahead or can't get buy-in from your team, try turning up your heat.

WARMTH **CHEAT SHEET**

WARMTH IN VOICE

▶ *Steady your breath*

▶ *Lower your tones*

▶ *Control your volume, showing good judgment about when to be soft and when to be louder*

▶ *Pause*

▶ *Inflect to draw in your audience*

WARMTH IN BODY LANGUAGE

▶ *Smile often*

▶ *Keep a soft, friendly gaze*

▶ *Make frequent eye contact, but don't stare*

▶ *Relax the face*

▶ *Lean forward*

▶ *Uncross the arms*

▶ *Point your feet toward your audience*

▶ *Hugs, warm handshake (if socially acceptable)*

WARMTH IN PRESENCE

▶ *Be receptive*

▶ *Acknowledge others*

▶ *Pursue active listening*

▶ *Stay humble*

- ▶ *Remain authentic*
- ▶ *Project respect*
- ▶ *Allow for vulnerability*
- ▶ *Find ways to convey relatability*
- ▶ *Project openness*

CHAPTER 7 | **TURN UP YOUR WARMTH**

EXTERNAL ASSESSMENT

Train Your Eyes

Begin by watching the people around you. Within professional settings, your social circle, and out on the street, watch for how people communicate warmth through their physical presentation and demeanor. How do they hold themselves and engage with the world around them?

Notice stance. Is it open or closed? Do people stand belly-to-belly, face-to-face, and with their feet toward you to communicate focused attention and engagement? Holding one's shoulders back with arms loosely at one's side communicates a disarming openness, whereas arms tightly folded or a body turned away says quite the opposite. Notice how an open and stiff stance can create a feeling of connectivity or a lack of it.

Notice eye contact. Who looks you in the eye? Who looks away? If the person you're speaking with isn't looking at you but surveying the room instead, how do you feel? Warm and fuzzy? Probably not.

NOTICE EXPRESSION. Occasionally and when appropriate, try to tune out the words people are saying and pay closer attention to their faces while they talk. A warm smile projects happiness in oneself and toward the person with whom they are interacting. The ability to look nonplussed and neutral even when rattled or agitated communicates both respect *and* warmth.

Turn Up Your Ears

When developing AWE-wareness of warmth in voice, listen to those around you. In your own relationships, consider whom you enjoy talking to. Whose voices put you at ease and conversely, on edge? Who is truly listening to you or the people in your group? Become more aware of how warmth sounds and how those audible cues make you feel.

NOTICE PITCH. Listen for warm tones and resonance, breath behind the words.

NOTICE PACE. People who speak very quickly and in run-on sentences lack warmth because they're not engaging their audience. They seem to be focused solely on their own output and want an audience that'll just listen. Conversely, individuals who pause and invite comment are regarded as warm and engaging.

NOTICE VOLUME. Lowering your cadence, audibly letting your guard down, and introducing a hint of vulnerability communicates warmth. Being generally soft and quiet, on the other hand, isn't necessarily warm but rather—hard to hear!

TAKE MENTAL NOTES. Who's letting their guard down? Who's relatable? The warmest people can make you feel like you're the only one in the room.

SELF-ASSESSMENT

Now it's your turn. Listen again to the recordings you made of your conversations with others throughout your day.

Assess Your Voice

Ask yourself: Is there audible warmth in my voice? Do I draw in my "audience" and put them at ease? Do I engage whomever I'm speaking to by inviting them into the conversation, or pausing long enough to allow them to reciprocate? Do I not only listen, but also hear what the other person is saying? Do I acknowledge them with words or nonverbal cues? If asked, could I repeat or mirror their words and cadence back to them?

Refer back to the Warmth Cheat Sheet on page 109 for a full description of warmth in voice. Ask for feedback: Do I communicate warmth in my voice? Do I audibly let my guard down and reveal some vulnerability? Do you feel drawn in when I speak and do you feel that I'm listening to you when *you* speak? Does my warmth sound authentic?

Fill in the blank: Today, I describe my voice as _____. On a scale of 1–5, I rate the level of warmth in my voice at _____.

Next,

Assess Your Body Language

Ask yourself: Do I smile as I speak? Do I make eye contact with the person I'm speaking to, or do I tend to look off, away, or down? Am I easy to laugh, or do I tend to have a serious expression, a poker face? Is my body language generally open or do I have a habit of crossing my arms and turning away in conversation?

Refer back to the Cheat Sheet on page 109 for a full description of warmth in body language and expression. Ask for feedback: Does my body language communicate warmth? Are my facial expressions warm or am I sometimes hard to read? Do I have a warm touch or do I create physical distance?

Fill in the blank: Today, I describe my body language as _____. On a scale of 1–5, I rate the level of warmth in my body language at _____.

Finally,

Assess Your Relatability

Do you come across as a generally warm person? When communicating with people, do you let your guard down enough to create a connection? Are you open, accessible, and allow yourself to be vulnerable? Do you let people see the *real you*, or at least a glimpse? Refer back to the Cheat Sheet on page 109 for a full description of warmth in relatability. And then assess how people are *reacting* to you. Ask yourself:

Do people seek out my company?

Do people sense my openness and open up to me?

Do people tend to trust me and follow my advice or direction?

Do people meet my gaze? Return my smile?

Do I receive more hugs than handshakes?

Or,

Do people approach me with some trepidation or caution?

Do I have a habit of interrupting and talking over?

Is it hard for me to relate with people?

Do people describe me as aloof, guarded, or hard to read?

Do people describe me as rigid or even defensive?

Do I have difficulty securing and retaining customers and employees?

Do I prefer to manage from the top down rather than through collaboration?

Do I get passed up for projects or promotions I'm technically qualified to do?

If you answered yes to any of the last eight questions, you may benefit greatly from improving your impression of warmth. Consider what specifically you could improve to be perceived and received more warmly. Changes to your voice? Body language? Wardrobe? General presence?

PRACTICE, PRACTICE, PRACTICE

Act the Part

Create connectivity through your body language and emotional expression. Whenever you speak with someone remember to:

Lean forward

Keep your arms uncrossed

Face your feet and body toward the person

Relax your face

Keep frequent eye contact

Smile when appropriate

Touch when appropriate

I tell my clients, if you want to practice warmth, go around hugging people with whom you already share a connection—using your best judgment and being careful about being appropriate. To be safe, I always let my female colleagues lead with the first hug. We've been working together so long, our office has a familial feel to it, so hugging is not unusual. It might be rarer where you work. Social psychologist Amy Cuddy says, "Don't fake it 'til you make it. Fake it 'til you become it." I couldn't agree more. If you aren't a hugger, and you spend the next three weeks embracing people—family members are a good choice—and generally being more physically open, you're going to *become* a warmer person. Where it might feel artificial at first, over time you will naturally change.

Speak Authentically

We all know or have encountered someone who lays it on a little too thick. They infuse warmth into their words for emotional effect to the point that we just don't buy it. I once coached a newscaster who could not shake what I called his "happy boy default." He would announce a terrible tragedy with geopolitical implications with the same cheery smile and perky voice he'd use to talk about a human-interest story about a family that had adopted twenty potbellied pigs. "You've got to stop that," I told him. "You're coming off as a phony. And if you're not believable, you're not credible."

I sometimes receive pushback on this point. Clients will insist, "I'm just being 'real'!" But you're not being real if you're *trying* to be real. In this case, it was like in an attempt to sound warm and relatable, he had shut off access to his sense of gravitas. The end result was a bit like a blue-suited Stepford wife. Once he was forced out of his comfort zone and became more willing to reveal a range of emotions, his speaking patterns started to evolve and align themselves more authentically with the content of his speech, deepening or rising and falling as appropriate. He smiled less frequently, but when he did, it felt like he meant it. His believability and authenticity increased his levels of warmth far more than a plastered-on smile ever could.

Deliver Inconsistency

Though often consistency is regarded as a positive characteristic or trait (I consistently show up for meetings on time, I consistently look people in the eye, I consistently build my client list), the opposite is true when you consistently deliver your words. In fact, consistency is the biggest killer to audible warmth. Do you always answer the phone the same way? (What's *up*?) Greet people with a standard line? (*Heeeeyyyy*, girlfriend.) Answer questions in a similar way? (You got it!) It's irritating to hear the same cloying answers when we ask someone how they're doing: "Couldn't be better," "No complaints," "All's good in the hood." With repeated use our signature "taglines" begin to sound disingenuous, as if we're speaking on automatic like Siri. The same old line delivered in the same old pitch, pace, and volume comes off as insincere. I know a guy who, when asked how he's doing, repeats his stock answer without fail, "Super! Never had a bad day in my life."

Really? Not one bad day, ever? This kind of consistent canned reply tells me I'm dealing with someone who would never willingly reveal vulnerability and thus can only make superficial connections. Trying to communicate with this kind of person is like talking to a friendly wall; you know whatever you say is unlikely to be absorbed.

Practice inconsistency. Drop your game face and your default delivery before your audience begins to distrust your intentions or what you're saying altogether. Vary your expressions to match how you authentically feel in the moment. You don't have to spill your whole life story to give honest answers. People respond poorly to predictability because it's inauthentic, so challenge yourself to add something *more* or *new* to your automatic responses in an effort to open up the conversation and engage in real dialogue. While people aren't particularly interested in hearing all the gory details of your problems, and it's generally better to be positive, a tiny bit of vulnerability (that is, "I got no sleep last night . . .") followed by a dollop of positivity (". . . but I'm on my fifth cup of coffee!) will always sound more real—and warmer—than "just another day in paradise."

Listen Deeply

It's always been my experience that you do learn more by listening than talking, and this became most apparent in improvisational theater class. In 2016, on a dare from my wife, I signed up for twelve weeks of improv training that culminated in an off-off-Broadway performance. This was way out of my comfort zone but what I took away from the experience was well worth the discomfort of performing on stage in Greenwich Village. The key to good improv, and any good conversation, is building upon what the last person says. In improv, actors are discouraged from saying, "No," which is a conversation stopper and instead encouraged to respond in both words and manner with "Yes, and . . ." This is the key to maintaining a back-and-forth exchange.

Up on stage, I learned pretty quickly that you cannot effectively add to the dialogue or overall story line unless you've been paying careful attention to what's just been said. An improv fail is when an actor has a deer-in-the-headlights moment, leaving words dangling in midair, waiting for a response. This shows a lack of attention on the part of the listener and can shut down a scene immediately. The same holds true in our public and private conversations. You cannot and will not sustain connection unless you're an effective listener.

The next time you're engaging in conversation, challenge yourself to do some deep listening to what the other person is saying. If they asked you to repeat their words right back to them, could you? Could you convey their perspective, along with their feelings, as they just described? As an additional tool to help you become a better listener, tune in to how people speak on television shows, in movies, and in theatrical settings.

I play a game when I watch television high-stakes dramas like *Homeland*, *The Americans*, and *Billions* in which I try to anticipate the next line of dialogue based on what was just previously said. All three of these shows are heavy on rapid-fire dialogue, which forces me to pay close attention and think fast. Of course, I never get the line right down to the word, but if I can get the gist then I know I'm really listening and I consider this a win. Imagine if all of us took a similar level of presence into our private and public conversations.

Hit the Pause Button

I once had a client who worked in sales and didn't understand why he was losing customers. Listening to the phone recordings of him doing business on the phone told me everything I needed to know. I told him, "You're a hard worker. You're smart, fast, and you're very skilled. But you will continue to lose out on opportunities until you start better acknowledging the other person. It's all output with you—talk, talk, talk. You're talking *at* people versus creating a connection that draws them *in*. How can you know what someone wants if you don't give them an opportunity to tell you?"

I handed him a stopwatch. "The next time you get on a sales call, start the watch. Give yourself only seven seconds max to speak and then pause."

It might sound contradictory, but creating space allows for more connection. Mastering *the pause* is one of the ways I made sure that I never repeated the mistake I made early in my career, when I chased away a potential client again by talking too much and listening too little. Now I make it a habit to take more "pause breaks" within my conversations. It allows me to read the room. How is my "audience" responding to me?

Pausing also creates space for the other person to interject and add their thoughts. Even if the person you're speaking with doesn't say anything in response to your pause, and simply nods or laughs, these nonverbal assertions still keep the conversation moving forward. Also, pausing doesn't mean you won't be able to finish your thought. A lot of people think that they're supposed to speak to the period—to the very end of a sentence before pausing. But it's often in mid-pause when the other person will say something that's tangential and additive to your point, which will further enhance the dialogue, reinforce your conversation, and boost the feeling of warmth between you. Pausing is a little thing, but it makes a big impact.

Are you a big talker? Story and joke teller? In your next meeting, take a "pause break" every few sentences or midsentence to allow your listener(s) a chance to reflect, as you make eye contact and nonverbally acknowledge them. It takes practice but if you habitually pause you'll avoid droning on and alienating people. Plus, the very act of stopping will invariably impact your own perspective on the mutuality and duality of healthy dialogue.

My client resisted my advice at first, but eventually he tried my stopwatch technique. A month later, he reported that he'd closed a record number of sales. In addition, he felt like he was feeling a positive shift in his personal relationships. I was thrilled, but not surprised. He was now balancing his output with other people's input. When you do that, you don't just more effectively communicate your message, you communicate respect, which in turn generates respect from others. The pause invites the person or people you're speaking with to reciprocate and *engage you*. His clients didn't realize it, but they were responding to the overall effect of heightened warmth.

Always Talk to Strangers

My wife, Raquel, teases me for making us late wherever we go because I stop and talk to everyone from point A to Z. I'm a natural extrovert and it's a big part of my job as an agent to facilitate conversations. Nearly every workday, I leave my office building at noon, walk down West Fifty-Sixth Street, pick up a salad, and walk back. This takes me twenty minutes, and in that short window of time, I look for simple ways to connect with people. As a college sports fan, I've memorized almost all the team nicknames of every university, so this is often my in. If I pass someone wearing a USC T-shirt, I might raise my fist and say, "Fight on!" If the guy standing next to me at the deli is wearing a Texas Longhorns hat, I may lean over and say, "Hook 'em." This simple gesture is always met with a smile and often leads to conversation because *people warm up to people who are warm to them.*

I also happen to love geography. In New York City, many taxi drivers hail from all over the world, and one of my favorite things to do when I catch a ride to the airport is to ask my driver where he or she is from. One day the answer was, "I'm from a small Central African country, Guinea." I said, "Really? You're from Guinea or Guinea-Bissau?" The driver went nuts. "I'm from Guinea-Bissau! I never tell anyone I'm from Guinea-Bissau because no one's ever even heard of it!" We ended up having this thirty-minute conversation about Guinea-Bissau. He was smiling broadly when I left the cab. I think it made his day that somebody actually cared enough to ask him about himself, someone who then knew something about his homeland.

This technique is not just about finding commonality; it's also a great way to learn. I know where I'm from. There's nothing interesting to me in talking about Hewlett, New York. But to get into a taxi and get to learn more about a tiny West African country, and make someone feel good because I took an interest in them, is a great way to spend a half hour. It's a practice that has enriched my life and makes my world a never-ending classroom.

It's about developing *relatability*. You can *always* find something in common with someone else. Because if you just think a little outside the box, they are like you. You could stick me in a room with someone anywhere on earth and give me about fifteen minutes and I could find something in common with that person. All I have to do is ask questions. Got kids? Got pets? Do you like meat? Do you not like meat? Do you like to work out? Do you like theater? Do you consider yourself an optimist or a pessimist? What do you think of sororities and fraternities? Where'd you grow up? Did you work on your school newspaper?

What's the last book you read? What video games do you play? All it takes is a little interest and effort.

Your relatability can be disarming in a way that totally warms you to the other person. And sometimes the more unexpected the connection is, the more relatable you'll become. As an example, I had a meeting scheduled with an executive who was originally from Birmingham, England. Beforehand, I did some research and I learned that, fun fact, Birmingham has a football club named Aston Villa. Cut to a week later, and halfway through our meeting, the exec mentioned that he was a soccer fan, so I casually said, "Oh yeah, are you an Aston Villa fan?" Well, he lit up like a firecracker, and talking soccer quickly became the highlight of our time together. All it takes is one single piece of common ground to create a connection.

The way I see it, the world is a giant playground and classroom for practicing your ability to connect. The point isn't to talk to *everyone*. Simply challenge yourself to strike up more conversations with "strangers" than you do now. Notice their reaction to you and your reaction in return. More often than not, surprising strangers with your curiosity and interest leads to connections that expand your network, friendships, business relationships, and overall understanding of the world. And though it may come easier for an extrovert like me, it only takes a minimum amount of effort to become more connected to the people around you.

As an added benefit, these connections can often lead to greater things. For example, in 1994, I was a guest at a wedding in Texas. The day before the big event, I was paired up with a cousin of the bride at a golf outing. We easily struck up a conversation. I learned he was from Toronto, and four hours later, he'd become my newest Canadian friend. Before the last hole, he suggested I get in touch with his neighbor, a twenty-seven-year-old guy who he believed could be a star in sports TV. On the advice of this stranger, when I got back to New York, I called his neighbor, who subsequently became one of my biggest clients and closest friends, ESPN's Dan Shulman.

OH, THE HUMANITY

A warm person creates a warm environment around them. Warmth invites vulnerability. If you're already a manager, you do that by building a team where it's okay to admit mistakes, to take risks, and to ask questions. But you can create this kind of work environment around you even if you're not already in a leadership or executive position. In fact, it's a great way to get noticed for those roles. You can be authoritative and nurturing. You show leadership as much when you accept constructive criticism and use it to take your work to the next level as you do when you deliver constructive criticism. The best leaders and leaders-in-training are willing to reveal their own humanity and allow others to be human and authentic around them, too (while laying down boundaries so they don't become the office therapist!). Give people the freedom to be who they are, and more often than not they'll give you back more than you—and sometimes even they—thought possible.

| ENERGY DRAWS THE WORLD IN

What do constitutional law, cage fighting, and hip replacements have in common? Nothing. Unless you're talking to someone who is fascinated by constitutional law, cage fighting, or hip replacements, in which case they have one thing in common—energy.

Truth is, you could say the same thing about cooking, chemical engineering, and landscape architecture. Marketing, yoga, and salsa dancing. Web design, woodworking, and accounting.

If you've ever tried something new—a recipe, a hobby, a sport, a career—because of another person's encouragement, you will understand what I'm talking about. We probably think we were influenced by the words the other person spoke when they mentioned the time spent outdoors, or the great exercise while having fun, or the way the activity soothes the spirit or sharpens the mind. Yet what we responded to in equal measure, whether we realized it or not, was the way the enthusiast's eyes lit up, the vigor in their voice, their animation when talking about this thing they found so interesting or exciting (surely *someone* lights up when they talk about accounting).

In short, we responded to their energy.

The Merriam-Webster dictionary lists several definitions for "energy." The first: "A dynamic quality." The last: "Usable power."

Yes. Energy, that dynamic quality, gives you power. The more energy you have, the more power you have to influence, to illuminate, to educate, or to engage. Authority earns other people's respect; warmth earns their affection and trust. Energy compels those people to follow.

Like the students in Barry Friedman's constitutional law class. For those unfamiliar with law school curricula, it's one of the biggest snoozer, as-boring-as-it-gets courses in any law program. As a first-year law student at Vanderbilt University, I, like all the other law freshmen, was required to take this class, and I was dreading it. That year, however, a new professor named Barry Friedman began teaching the course. Not ten minutes into his first lecture, I was captivated. This waif of a man spoke with such conviction, though I was sitting in a class of eighty people it felt like he was speaking directly to me. He started off slow and easy, saying something to the effect of "People, the United States of America is the greatest country on earth." And then he built up from there, his words coming faster, his volume rising as he traveled back and forth across the floor, using his whole body to emphasize important words: "But do you realize, you are ONE step away from losing your freedom? The ONLY thing that separates you and me from prison . . . is the Fourth Amendment." Every lecture was a constitutional law version of "Stairway to Heaven," a song that built to a crescendo as he drummed his words into his students with such animation and heart he practically roused all of us out of our seats. "I'm calling on you. Wake up. This is AMERICA." He was in the aisles. He sat on the desk. In some classes apparently he stood on the desk. His energy was *off the charts*, allowing him to do the unthinkable—make the stalest material fascinating and inspiring. As soon as I could, I signed up for every single class that Professor Friedman taught.

When I caught up with him to ask if he was conscious of how he infused such energy into his material, he said, "First I have to tell you a funny story, and it has to do with me not being energetic.

"The first case I ever tried was in the United States Supreme Court and I was the second chair, next to a mentor of mine who was a terrific trial lawyer. I prepped my first witness for the stand and I put him on, and when we were done and we were walking back to the office I asked my mentor, 'How'd I do?' And he said, 'You did great, but you might have thought about using your body and voice, moving around closer to the witness, farther from the witness—just to kind of keep everybody on their toes.' And I realized that what I'd done on a hot afternoon in the courtroom after everybody had just had lunch, was to just sit there monotone, going on for hours asking one question after the other. I'd put everybody to sleep.

"I thought this was a great lesson and it's one I teach young lawyers all the time now, which is that *you can actually control a room with your energy.* By thinking about how you use your body and projecting your excitement and your enthusiasm into your voice, you can actually spark up the place."

It's good advice not just for up-and-coming lawyers. Friedman uses his energy to control a classroom, but you can use your energy to control any room, from a conference room to a corner office to a cubicle. Forget the room—you can use it to control any engagement, no matter where you are or how few people you're talking to.

Lawrence Epstein knows this. Epstein is COO of the multi-billion-dollar Ultimate Fighting Championship (UFC), the largest mixed–martial arts promotion company in the world. Combining disciplines like boxing, Brazilian jujitsu, karate, wrestling, Thai wrestling, judo, and tae kwon do, mixed martial arts brings together athletes to fight in an octagonal "cage," in reality an open-topped chain-link fence, albeit with little give. Early on, with few rules or safety precautions like gloves or weight categories, the sport was unregulated and cultivated a reputation as a "no-holds barred spectacle of brutality." It was banned in thirty-six states, making it difficult for UFC to host events, and barred from cable TV. Enter Lawrence Epstein, a tall, classically good-looking forty-year-old managing partner at Las Vegas–based Beckley Singleton. "I watched Bruce Lee and karate movies as a kid," said Epstein, "and growing up in Las Vegas, I loved boxing." So he liked the fights, but he'd never planned to deviate far from the traditional lawyering path. Yet when given the chance, though at the top of his professional game, he took a huge risk by leaving Beckley Singleton to join the controversial sports upstart as its in-house counsel. He recounts his first interaction with UFC 1 (the very first UFC fight): "I was blown away by the spectacle. The fight was a sumo wrestler versus a Dutch savateur, a kickboxer. The sumo guy was just this huge, giant dude, and he ended up getting his tooth knocked out and beat in a minute or less. [It was better than that—one of the sumo wrestler's teeth wound up somewhere in the audience, and the other two were embedded so deep in the Dutchman's foot the doctors decided it was safer to just wrap the foot up and let him fight rather than try to get them out on the spot.] I was like, 'I can't believe what I just saw. That was *crazy*. It was exciting and provocative and had that 'holy shit' factor. But I could also see how the sport could be respected, could be regulated, could be legitimate and become part of the permanent sports landscape. It felt like a historic opportunity. It was a completely new challenge, and I sunk my teeth into it."

Epstein soon made his mark effecting transformational growth in the organization, not through any brilliant legal strategy, but by leveraging risk and maximizing his relentless enthusiasm for the sport into a campaign to build positive recognition of Ultimate Fighting.

"We literally went door to door to door to door and changed people's minds," recounts Epstein. The doors he's talking about are the ones in the state legislatures where he spent hours talking to legislators, working to convince them that the company had gone above and beyond to implement rules that would make it the safest martial art in the world. "We were a disruptor in sports space and we had a lot of critics, but we knew that the facts were on our side. All we had to do was get people to listen. We knew we created significant economic impact every time we did an event. We knew we had a rabid fan base that loved us. We knew that our athletes were special people, most of them college-educated because they came out of wrestling programs, and all of them martial artists with a central tenet of respect and discipline and sportsmanship. And then, there was our safety record. We'd done almost nine thousand fights and we'd never had a serious injury. Slowly," Epstein said, "we built a coalition of people that were supportive, and then that support gained momentum."

Epstein's energy for building the UFC eventually caught fire, inspiring a growing fan base worldwide.

"The key to keeping the process moving forward was just relentless optimism."

It took twenty years, but in 2016, when New York finally lifted its ban, MMA became legal in all fifty states.

"It felt like we won the Super Bowl or the World Series," recalled Epstein. "There was this very tangible sense of not just accomplishment, but winning."

The live title fight between Eddie Alvarez and Conor McGregor at Madison Square Garden on November 12, 2016, broke every UFC record, including a crowd of more than fifteen thousand for the prefight *weigh-in*!

Let's remember that Epstein was not following a dream here. He wasn't born with a passion to make the world love mixed martial arts. Rather, he ascribes his success to choosing to be "all in," to whatever it is that he's doing in the moment. When it was representing casinos and boxing companies in Las Vegas, he was into casinos and boxing companies. Once he committed to representing MMA, he got into MMA. I'm sure he would have given the same energy to car manufacturers or the fragrance industry if that's where his career had taken him. As he says, "You manufacture your own passion. There has to be a desire to get into the details. You should want to be the most knowledgeable about whatever you are going to do. Think about how rewarding it is when you learn about something and help someone . . . it makes you dig deeper." As soon as you start talking to Epstein about the sport, you can feel his passion. This is what he does; this is what he cares about and he is *into it*. When you listen to somebody who's this passionate about something they've built, you can't not be interested in it. There's no other way Epstein could have persisted. Most successful people have a focus and passion that translates to high energy. Energy is key to Epstein's ability to inspire and persuade. "People say, 'How can you devote your life to people fighting in a cage? What kind of life is that?' I LOVE IT . . . that type of energy that only comes from being all in."

Never underestimate the power of your commitment to your message or idea. It can turn skeptics into converts.

I'm a lot like Lawrence Epstein and Barry Friedman in that whatever I get into, I want to get everyone else into it as well. Recently it's been hips. By the time you're reading this, I'll have gotten two new hips, but not before I read pretty much everything there is to read about hips. I'm passionate about the subject now. I've watched videos of hip resurfacing, and can quote studies that explain why the procedure isn't recommended for women. Give me enough time with this topic and I could become a hip surgeon. But more to the point, I'm so intrigued by this topic that given enough time I might be able to convince *you* to become a hip surgeon. As with most things in my life, I choose to be *into it*. You could throw me into a chewing gum factory and I'd learn every single thing there is to know about gum and make it my mission to show you why gum is the greatest thing on earth. It's just what I do, because the alternative, to plod through life wishing you were somewhere else or doing something else, seems like an awful waste of time. But curiosity is not enough to create energy. Curiosity combined with a desire to learn *and* a desire to share—that's energy.

ENERGY BUILDS CONNECTIONS

The components of energy are conviction, enthusiasm, engagement, and emotional commitment to your message. When you believe in and trust what you're saying, your audience inevitably will, too. You must be genuinely all in—present, authentic, and fully engaged. Individuals with a strong emotional commitment have no trouble motivating and influencing people because they simultaneously make an emotional *connection*. That's why people like Barry Friedman and Lawrence Epstein are so successful. From the moment they meet you, whether in the halls of a capitol building or a university classroom, they are creating a relationship. They're looking you in the eyes, acknowledging you, gauging what you need at that moment. Like a Jehovah's Witness at your doorstep, they know they've got one chance to get your attention and get you to open the door and welcome them in. That's what Barry Friedman is doing as he waltzes across the classroom, sending out his energy in the hope that it's contagious. Once he's got your attention, he can use other tools at his disposal to make sure you have a deep understanding of what he's trying to teach you and why it matters, not just in general, but to *you*. Epstein did the same thing when he walked the halls of state legislatures trying to get lawmakers to move beyond their preconceived ideas about the sport he loved. Persuasion and understanding cannot happen without first building an initial relationship. We do the same dance on a micro level every day of our lives, especially in a work environment where we need people to pay attention to our thoughts and ideas if we want to move forward professionally or have a positive impact. That only happens when we can get others as committed, or at least as accepting and open to our goals or ideals, as we are.

ENERGY AND WARMTH WORK TOGETHER

Though energy and warmth overlap, they can operate separately. Have you ever been in the presence of someone who is revved up and excited, but completely uninterested or unaware of what anyone else around them is doing or feeling? That's what energy with low warmth looks like. An employee beloved by all who never gets the promotion is probably someone with extraordinary levels of warmth but not enough energy to convince superiors they're good leadership material. They can get people to like them, but there's no evidence they can get people to follow.

Josie Thomas, executive vice president and chief diversity and inclusion officer of CBS Corporation, doesn't have either problem. In addition to overseeing the diversity issues across the entire CBS broadcast division, Showtime, and Simon & Schuster publishing, Thomas is also the company ambassador in dealing with advocacy groups from the far left to the far right, including the LGBTQ community and Focus on the Family, and everyone in between. Before America elected the first African-American president or voted for legalizing gay marriage, Thomas was effectuating this kind of sociological and societal change within one of the country's largest and most influential media giants. How does she manage to handle so many different and passionate constituencies who often represent polarizing subjects?

Thomas is the ideal amalgam of AWE. Her authority credentials speak for themselves, but to achieve that perfect blend of warmth and energy, she says she keeps in mind one of her mother's favorite quotes, by Maya Angelou: "'People will forget what you said. People will forget what you did. But people will never forget how you made them *feel*.' This quote epitomized Mother completely because everyone who knew her felt very important in her space, and this became the standard for me." The way Thomas warmly acknowledges her "audience" and energetically punctuates her rapid-fire vocal delivery with a joyful laugh envelops and draws you in. You just can't help but to feel good in her presence, even when she's kicking your ass.

Before Thomas was in her current job, she was the lead attorney for CBS News, and I found myself on the other side of the negotiating table with her repeatedly. Even when she sometimes refused to accede to my demands, her warm, energetic delivery left everyone in the room feeling good about what had just happened. Let's say you wanted $5 million for your client. She might come back with an offer of $500,000. But when she did, she would explain to you why $500,000 was actually a great offer, and why it was truly in the best interest of your client to accept it. And the way she said it, she conveyed that while she was always going to put the needs of her client first, it mattered to her that whatever happened in that negotiating room was right and ethical. Of course she could just tell you to take the offer or leave it—and I suspect she would if she had to—but in all of my interactions with her, she first took the time to try to make sure you and your client walked away feeling respected.

"I've always tried to incorporate acknowledgment into my business style because you can't motivate people otherwise," says Thomas. "You just won't get the best results by deflating people and making them feel as if they're not important. People are constantly trying to create small circles to exclude people who are different than they are, but to build the strongest companies with the most productive work environments, we *must* create larger circles to include everyone. And for me," she continues, "This is about fairness. You exist. I exist. Inherently, everyone needs to be acknowledged."

ENERGY REQUIRES ALIGNMENT AND ATTUNEMENT

Again, we're talking about input and output. We generally think of energy as something we put out into the world, good or bad, but you can actually deflate people with too much energy. If Professor Friedman were standing on the desk during every class, it would feel like you were attending a Metallica concert, not law school. You'd likely feel assaulted, get tired of the shtick, and eventually start to ignore him. Just as warmth demands acknowledging others, good energy demands acknowledging and drawing out other people's energy. It's something Howard Stern learned to tremendous effect. Once known as a shock jock who berated and humiliated his guests, after years of intense psychotherapy he now conducts long, thoughtful interviews, what the *New York Times* called "character excavations," on Sirius satellite radio. He has learned to balance the output with the input. Part of that is learning to listen better (warmth) but it's also that, as the *Times* wrote, "his interest in people has never had greater depth or range." When you give people room for input, and use warmth to acknowledge them, you grow energy between you, which always makes for better relationships at work and in your private life. Modulate your energy in response to the overall energy of the room and you easily become the person whom everybody loves talking to and working with. The secret to having just the right amount of energy is not an exact science. It's more of a *feeling*. Michael Borkow, a former writer for *Roseanne* who ascended to head writer on *Friends*, explains that you must first read the room if you want to win the room. After all, even a great comedian can fail in the wrong crowd.

"In Hollywood, I can think of a surprising number of people who have gotten fired from jobs on writing staffs and it's not because people didn't think they were talented; it's because they weren't right for that room. It could be that they had too much energy or they had the *wrong* kind of energy. I can think of someone who was fired from a show because he brought a frat boy energy to the room and infected all the other guys with that frat boy energy. The showrunner didn't want that energy in his room. The writer was an extremely energetic guy and that was a liability in that situation." In this case, the writer literally wasn't reading the room properly, and therefore couldn't modulate his energy to match what was needed at the time. Even if you don't work in the creative petri dish that is a comedy writers' room, everyone has to collaborate at some point. You have to know how to engage in whatever room you happen to be in. It's about knowing when to step up, step back, and allow *everyone's* energy to coalesce rather than making things all about you. When you are consumed with making everything about you, you can't put out good energy or make room for that of others. When you are consumed with *worry* that everything is about you, you shortchange yourself and those around you the same way. Stop thinking about yourself so much and you'll find a lot more freedom to simply be yourself.

An energetic connector is like a great performer. It's impossible to be in their presence without becoming intoxicated by their vibe. Now, this isn't to say you have to be larger than life to make your point. You have to be authentically *you* to be authentically compelling. People can smell a fake; your audience will know in an instant if your energy is artificial or insincere.

A TRULY RENEWABLE RESOURCE

As indefinable as energy is, we can execute it in very definable ways: through Voice, Body Language, Presence, Authenticity, and a sense of Service.

Voice

When we use our voice to build trust with warmth, we acknowledge and we listen. By acknowledging and listening, we also learn what other people need. Warmth allows you to read the room so you can present with the level of energy others need to feel their best in your presence. Speaking with warmth is like enveloping someone in a metaphorical hug; speaking with energy envelops people in your unwavering belief in your own message. If you've read the room correctly, whether it's a room of one or one hundred, they'll likely be open to it. Add in Authority and you've not just read the room, you've won it.

It can take work. Christopher Russo has been on the air more than thirty-five years, first as the "Mad Dog" half of the insanely popular New York sports radio show *Mike and the Mad Dog*, and for the last decade on his own show on Sirius satellite radio, *Mad Dog Unleashed*. He's like the Jack Russell terrier of sports radio— more energetic and more frenetic than anyone else in his category, starting at 10 and ending at 10. "Passion and energy is what draws people in. It's contagious and the more the better," says Russo. "Enthusiasm sells. No question about it. People want to hang around an enthusiastic person." It's true. Russo might say, "How the hell can the Mets make that trade? That's CRAZY! That's a CRAZY trade!" And if you happened to be listening, whether you liked the Mets or not you'd probably find yourself nodding and thinking, "Sheesh, how *could* the Mets make that trade?" The thing is, Russo happens to love talking about sports, but with that kind of energy, he could be talking about vacuum cleaners and you'd still idle in your parking spot to postpone getting out of your car until he was finished speaking. You're not riveted because of the volume of his voice—which is pretty loud—you're caught because his pitch and pacing are so surprising, you don't know what to expect next. It's that element of surprise that keeps you in your car.

Now, like a Jack Russell terrier who isn't getting enough attention and exercise, someone who's always at 10 would be exhausting to be around all the time when he's not on the radio. Russo has learned over the course of his long career to modulate his energy when he shifts from speaking to an audience of millions down to one. "You really have to be perceptive about that. I can overpower my family at the dinner table. My twelve-year-old isn't used to all that noise. There are certain places where high energy works and others where you're better off tuning it down, and with experience you learn how to do that. In real life, when you're off the air, you have to pick your spots."

Everyone can "pick their spots." You don't need to aim for talk show or radio host level in your enthusiasm and energy; you just need to allow your interest in whatever the topic at hand is to show. Whatever you do, however, don't pretend. Faking interest, pandering to people, will backfire on you in a heartbeat. If warmth is the seed for relationships, energy is the water that keeps it growing.

Body Language

Those who deliver a sense of conviction and passion audibly with their words almost always exhibit energetic body language, too, in the form of expressive hand movements, emotive facial expressions, and a larger-than-life physical presence.

Not only does heightened energy increase our overall AWE, but research shows that it also boosts our likability. Professor Frank Bernieri of Oregon State University points to a behavioral principle called the "expressivity halo," where people who communicate in an expressive, animated fashion tend to be liked more than difficult-to-read people. We're just more comfortable around people with whom we have a strong connection, and understanding how people feel creates connection.

In terms of being easy to read and rating high on the likability scale, I can't think of a better example than the insanely popular veteran sportscaster Dick Vitale, who is over eighty years old and nonetheless runs circles around his thirty-year-old competitors. If energetic people are surrounded by an expressivity halo, Vitale's halo must rival that of the archangel Gabriel.

Vitale, known by many as "Dickie V," not only speaks with high audible energy, but also he expresses unfettered, physical energy. His hands are never still. When they're not clasping and unclasping in front of him, they either swoop up and around and to the side like they're trying to physically move Vitale's words around, or they form a bobbing parenthesis, as though they're trying to frame his thoughts as they come out. And that's when he's calm. He becomes so animated when he calls a game, you're expecting to see his words explode out of his mouth. My wife, who's never been overly interested in basketball, will, however, sit through a good stretch of the game to hear Vitale's signature catchphrase—*This is AWESOME, baby!* He electrifies and rouses his fans as if he's just given everyone in the stands a five-hour energy shot. Hundreds of thousands of these fans also follow him daily for his motivational "life" tips of the day that extend beyond the court.

"I tell people, if you don't have a passionate sense of pride and a passion about what you're doing, you're not going to be a success. So, find something you love to do. No matter what I've done, I've tried to do it with *energy, enthusiasm,* and an *excitement.* And I really try to utilize all three in my everyday approach."

ESPN recently awarded him with a lifetime contract, a move signaling that the network also doesn't see Vitale slowing down anytime soon.

"I told [ESPN], nobody's gonna have to tell me when it's over," Vitale told me in the spring of 2018. "If I lose that drive and desire and passion to go out and do a game, I'll be the first to pick up the phone and say, 'Hey, it's been a great run.'" He still hasn't lost the passion, and is probably more enthusiastic now than ever, given what he told the *New York Post* in March 2019: "I'm tellin' ya: I want to be the first guy in history to walk in and do a game when I'm 100 years old. And stand and say: *'This is awesome, baby! With a capital A!'"*

AWEsome indeed.

Presence

Creating connections is Andrew Slabin's superpower. By his own admission, he is not the smartest guy in the aforementioned room. "I got all of my accomplishments through EQ [emotional quotient, i.e. emotional intelligence]." Spend two seconds in his presence and it's also undeniable that much of Slabin's success can be attributed to the sheer force of his *energy*. He smiles and laughs easily, and is quick to turn the joke on himself. An eccentric dresser who's often outfitted like Thurston Howell, he'll also don a ball cap at Fenway Park. He's a prodigiously funny and fast-talking storyteller, and he easily wins any room by infecting his audience with his good humor and zealous presence.

An unimpressive high school student, Slabin says, "I always had to work a little harder than the next guy," and credits his "scrappy hustler" work ethic for landing an internship at John Hancock Mutual Funds in Boston while still in college. "I worked my ass off. While everyone else was traveling around Europe, I spent my summers in the office doing credit write-ups and learning all that I could. They invited me back when I graduated. I was the only intern they ever hired who didn't have an MBA."

After a successful five and a half years at John Hancock, Slabin moved to New York, where the famed Merrill Lynch media analyst Jessica Reif took Slabin under her wing. Another five years later, his success at Merrill propelled him into a portfolio manager position at the world's biggest hedge fund, GLG Partners, where he worked directly for the firm's billionaire founder, Noam Gottesman. Every step of the way, Slabin won over influential power brokers up and down Wall Street who made him their protégé. After a two-decade run in the hedge fund world, Slabin decided to pivot his career. With no experience or résumé for the job, he transitioned to his current role as executive vice president of global investor strategy at media giant Discovery Communications, working for CEO David Zaslav. "I had to convince the headhunter to put me in the queue. They wouldn't hire me because I didn't have IR [investor relations] experience. They didn't want to put a square into a circle. I said I've never done IR, but I've consumed it as a customer for over twenty years. Think about me differently." He didn't have the requisite credentials, experience, or authority for the job, and there were likely many more qualified candidates that represented lower risk, but he intoxicated his headhunter with enthusiasm, even though she originally wanted a circle in a circle. Then he convinced the next person with whom he interviewed. Then the CFO. Finally, Zaslav.

Is it simply scrappy hard work that allowed Slabin to soar beyond expectations? He doesn't think so. "You can be the smartest guy in the world, but [it doesn't matter] if you can't communicate your ideas. It's imperative to be able to work with people. Discovery was concerned that I'd never worked with a traditional company [as opposed to investment firms]. It made me think about how you do that. How do you influence without authority? How do you bring people together?"

At a recent annual review, the CFO of Discovery told Slabin he was among the best hires he'd made in his twenty-year career, not only because he's been an integral part of the management team that acquired Scripps Networks in his first few weeks on the job, but also because Slabin's the guy you want to get stuck next to on a delayed plane. Or at a long convention. Or the company dinner party. One of Slabin's old bosses would regularly sit him next to celebrities and other heavyweight guests at company events because he never fails to energize the crowd—no matter who is in it. If they had Oscars for contagious energy he would be walking the red carpet annually. There were many other candidates who could have made money for the company; only Slabin had the right energy to build the relationships that would elevate the stock price.

Service

If you think about it, a commitment to service seems to be a primary source of energy for many of the people we've met in this chapter. Professor Friedman, Lawrence Epstein, Josie Thomas, Mad Dog Russo, Dick Vitale—all excel at what they do because of their commitment to serving their "audience." Mike Novogratz is cut from the same cloth. When he walks into a room, he immediately captures your attention. He's a walking paradox able to inhabit two seemingly disparate worlds at the same time. The former college wrestler and ex-military vet is still chiseled in his fifties, and so impeccably groomed he could be mistaken for a professional stylist. He lives an aristocratic lifestyle, inhabiting a majestic Manhattan mansion in the sky, yet still maintains the common touch as one of seven children raised in a middle-class Catholic family. He can be boisterous and energetic, but because he also carries himself with virtually no self-consciousness, he emanates a contagious lightness.

When I first met Novogratz, he was excited to share with me a deep breathing technique he'd recently learned on a trip to India. I quickly obliged because, *why not?* And within a matter of seconds, I forgot that he's one of the youngest partners in the history of the esteemed Wall Street firm Goldman Sachs; the founder of the macro and liquid markets business at Wall Street powerhouse Fortress Investment Group; and the founder of Galaxy Digital LP, a leader in the emerging world of cryptocurrency. For more than a decade, Novo (as he's called on the Street) has ridden the tumultuous highs and lows of the stock market and rebounded every time. Today Novo has made more than $1 billion in the crypto space and is considered among the sharpest cryptocurrency traders and investors. Yeah, the same guy demonstrating breathing techniques in an easy chair.

Even if I hadn't arrived for an interview, it wouldn't have occurred to me to refuse his invitation to try his new breathing technique, despite how awkward it felt. When he talks to you, you believe that whatever it is he's excited about is something that you're going to be excited about, too. This is why Novogratz is so successful—he has an energy about him that inspires and motivates people to consider new ideas and take risks. He admits as much.

"I'm a good trader. We navigated this last chapter in crypto very well, but my real success is being able to *energize* the crowd."

He does this, he explains, by turning the focus off of himself, a "trick" he emulated from motivational speaker Tony Robbins. He likes to tell the story of when he was asked to go to Switzerland and speak to a group of investors.

"I got there and there were six hundred people, big TVs, and—I had a panic attack. I literally couldn't calm myself down. I was the keynote speaker and I was quaking. I went into the bathroom and I said to myself, 'Why is Tony Robbins so good at this and you're such a weenie right now? Why are you so scared?' I couldn't answer the question, so I decided to *just be Tony*. I asked for a walking mic and I went onstage and told a funny joke and became Tony Robbins. All of a sudden I was able to get into rhythm and calm down, and I gave a great speech.

"I met Tony about six months later, and I told him this story about how I'd stolen his persona and it had saved me in that moment of personal peril. And he said something to me that I'll never forget. He said, 'Why do you think I don't get nervous?' He said, 'Life's about service and if you go onstage thinking, how do I serve the audience, then it's no longer about you.'"

"[Tony] helped me realize that I was nervous because I was worried about *myself*," Novogratz continued. "I was thinking, *what are they going to think about me?* It was all ego and I had to let it go. Now, when I go onstage talking about crypto, I make it about [the audience], not me. I look at how I can impart some wisdom, make people feel better, do something to serve their community—this defines what you talk about."

Since flipping the script and focusing less on the impression he's making, Novo has discovered that he's not only less nervous to address a crowd, but also he's more *energized* by a greater sense of service. By focusing your attention on your audience and the material you're presenting, you tap into a reservoir of energy that's deeply engaging.

"The moment you realize that it's an honor to be onstage and an opportunity to serve [your audience]," says Novo, "you win the room. And not through manipulation, but with sincerity."

Sincerity is key. Novogratz is unfailingly authentic and doesn't hold back; he approaches everyone with an abundance of energy that's extraordinarily charismatic and compelling, and he does it consistently. It's one skill to make a strong favorable first impression; it's another thing entirely to live up to that impression over and over again. People feel good energy right away, particularly when bolstered by warmth. They feel comfortable and trusting. The real skill is being able to sustain that energy so that people continue to believe and trust in you through repeated interactions, to prove through your actions that your energy is not just a shtick, that you're not just saying the words they want to hear. That your goal is to do your best to deliver the end result you have led them to hope for, whether it's a successful quarter, a team-oriented work environment, or the freedom to take risks without fear.

The best in business approach their work with the same intensity and attention to detail and craft as the most skilled artisan. If you haven't already, cultivate a deep desire to learn, explore, and serve, and wear it on your sleeve. You'll find it naturally infuses you with an infectious energy that draws others to you, making them receptive to your message whether you're trying to reach one or one hundred.

CHAPTER 9 | **TURN UP YOUR ENERGY**

*In the last chapter we learned that Professor Barry Friedman some-*times stood on his desk to get his students' attention and impress them with his energy. Your goal should be to exude that kind of energy, too, even when you have no desk, and even when you're not in performance mode. Not all the time, of course. It's exhausting to be "on" all the time, for you and for the people around you. But it's equally exhausting, for others, anyway, if you are *never* on. In either case, you wind up draining other people's energy, either by overwhelming them or forcing them to work too hard to engage with you. Once you start monitoring your energy levels in your voice, body language, and presence and modulating them according to the needs of your audience, you will be amazed at the improvement you'll see in the way strangers and friends alike respond to you. For the people inter-acting with you, it's the difference between riding the kiddie train at the amusement park or riding the roller coaster. In one, you sit back, look out the side, and after a while, tune out. If you're over the age of two, there's nothing to grab your attention or make the ride memorable. However, you can't help but be present and engaged on the roller coaster. You're clutching the safety rail or flinging your arms up into the air, your heart is racing, there is no checking out—you are paying attention! And when you get off the ride, you're smiling and looking forward to doing it all over again. While you probably don't want to be so over-the-top you give people whiplash, if your energy keeps people engaged and present during your interactions, you'll always make an indelible impression.

EXTERNAL ASSESSMENT

Turn Up Your Ears

Listen to identify those with energy around you. Who injects energy, enthusiasm, and emotional commitment into their message? Who is creating a contagion with their ideas? Audible energy can be highly motivating, although it sometimes needs to be modulated to match the temperature of the room.

Listen for people who speak to, not *at*, their audience. Also listen for those who acknowledge their crowd of 1–100 and invite them into the conversation. Conversely, listen for people who flood the room with their energy and suck up all the air. This is an example of deflating energy. Individuals who breathe energy back into the room often do so by acknowledging and listening to their audience *even as they're speaking.*

NOTICE PITCH. Inflection is infection. When you inflect with your voice and vary your vocal intonations, you infect the listener with unpredictable energy.

NOTICE PACE. People who ramble and run through stop signs with their words are often perceived as too high-energy and out of attunement with their audience. They're also predictable, which is boring. Energy does not equal speed.

NOTICE VOLUME. Loud doesn't necessarily communicate energy. Think of the preschool teacher who uses a very low voice during a pre-nap story time. She doesn't yell or scream, yet the variation in her cadence and energy keep the children 100 percent engaged.

Take a Look Around

Those who have a passion, a desire, and drive for what they do have energy about them that almost inevitably energizes their audience. When developing AWE-wareness of energy in body language, keep an eye out for people who outwardly express their inner enthusiasm. The giveaway is emotive body language.

TAKE NOTES. Who speaks with their hands and body? Who makes sure they're connecting with their "audience"? Is the audience nodding, as if to say, "Tell me more"? Or do they look bored or even overwhelmed? No matter how emotionally committed a person is to their message, if they don't also engage their audience, they'll lose their attention. Some of the most effective energetic connections come from having the insight and the wherewithal to know that your energy is not overwhelming or deflating others around you. Put up your antennae. With some practice and observation, you'll know you're in the presence of uplifting energy when your own energy level begins to rise.

SELF-ASSESSMENT

One more time, listen to the recordings you made of your conversations throughout your day, and think about how you behaved and interacted as you spoke.

Assess Your Voice

Ask yourself: Do I convey enthusiasm with my voice? When I speak, do people pay attention? Do my words and message tend to engage, and even excite, my audience? How well do I modulate my audible energy to match, or attune to, my audience? Am I speaking at my audience, or acknowledging them as I speak and then inviting them into the conversation? Do I allow for an exchange of energy rather than being solely focused on my own output?

Refer back to the Cheat Sheet on page 73 for a full description of how energy is delivered through voice. Ask for feedback from your "scout": Would you describe my pace as slow, fast, or somewhere in the middle? How would you describe my tone and use of vocal variety? Do I inflect as I speak and add punch to certain words for emphasis? Do my words tell a story and keep my audience entertained and engaged? Or do my stories sometimes fall a little flat? Do I speak as if I'm emotionally committed to my message? Does my enthusiasm about my subject energize others? (Think: Professor Friedman controlling the classroom with his energy.)

Fill in the blank: Today, I describe my voice as _____.
On a scale of 1–5, I rate the level of energy in my voice at _____.

Assess Your Body Language

Ask yourself: Am I emotive? Do I use my hands to underscore my message?

Does my body language express my passion and inner enthusiasm? (Think Dick Vitale stirring up the fans.) Do I use a range of facial expressions to engage my audience and communicate Vitale's "three E's" of life—energy, enthusiasm, and excitement?

Refer back to the Cheat Sheet on page 73 for a full description of how energy is delivered through physical expression. Ask for feedback: How would you describe my body language? Energized, or a bit droopy, or stiff? Does my expression of outward energy seem authentic, or more like a show?

Fill in the blank: Today, I describe my body language as _____. On a scale of 1–5, I rate the level of energy in my physical gestures and expressions at _____.

Assess Your Presence

Does your energy tend to energize other people? Do people feel your inner drive? (Think Lawrence Epstein's relentless passion for his sport.) Refer back to the Cheat Sheet on page 73 for a full description of energy in presence. And then assess how people are *reacting* to you:

Do I generally hold people's attention?

Do people get excited by what I have to say?

Do people get excited by my willingness to take risks?

Do I often inspire and motivate people to take action?

Do I use humor to energize and relate to my audience?

Can I easily motivate people to do XYZ?

Does my energy feel authentic?

Or,

Is my energy sometimes too BIG and off-putting?

Is my energy sometimes too low-key and boring?

Am I sometimes hard to relate to?

Do I have difficulty reading the room?

Do I have difficulty modulating my energy to match my audience?

Do I give the impression that I'm all about ME, instead of about you?

Do I get passed up for projects or promotions I'm technically qualified to do?

Consider what specifically you could change to give a more energetic impression. Changes to your voice? Body language? General presence?

TIPS FOR ADDING ENERGY

We've all been stuck on an airplane, at a dinner party, or waiting in line with someone who drones on. They mumble, their voice so dull and lacking in punch you wish you could turn their volume *all* the way down. Slow and low worked great for Mr. Rogers because he was talking to small children, who are still learning to absorb information and make sense of the world. Talk like that to grown-ups and you'll put them to sleep.

You can speak with spark through inflection and variation.

Play with Pace

When Mike Corey, a play-by-play broadcaster with ESPN specializing in football, basketball, and lacrosse, sought out our coaching, we focused on his energy. He was like Barry Friedman on steroids, talking too much on and off the air and alienating the very people he wanted to impress, the very people who held his career in their hands. He was hungry to announce the nationally televised Saturday night games, but he kept getting assigned the ones airing on Tuesday. The squeaky wheel gets the grease unless people get used to the squeak and tune it out; Mike's ambition and insecurity was causing him to ramp up his energy in a totally unproductive fashion that turned people off and pushed them away. We had to figure out how to redirect his energy so that he could draw his bosses to him and help them recognize that he deserved to be mentored, supported, and promoted even without him blasting the message in their faces.

While he had a deep and rich voice, Corey spoke in a lot of run-on sentences, which made his voice sound monotone. He wasn't even aware that he tended to be a bit dull and windy. I suggested he use fewer words and insert more frequent pauses into his speech. Long-winded talkers are a bit like sprinters— they don't know how to slow down, but they do know how to stop. By forcing himself to halt after every seven seconds of speech with either full stops or elongated pauses—the stop-watch exercise we discussed in Chapter 7—he built in time for his audience to reciprocate and participate in the dialogue without pouncing on their words, so the conversation could flow better. Counterintuitively, you can actually say more when you slow down. The key, however, is eye contact. As you pause, your eye contact allows you to alert the person you're speaking with that you're not quite done and helps them not zone out, somewhat in the way changing traffic lights keep drivers alert and prepared to stop, slow down, or speed up. Between your pacing and your eye contact, you help keep the energy going between you and you give them a chance to let you know they're following you with a nod or a small interjection like "uh-huh." That little break makes all the difference between a monologue and a productive, energized dialogue. When Corey tried this technique, his delivery was completely transformed, turning him into a more authoritative speaker who modulated his energy as the situation warranted and gave other people time to express themselves. He felt the difference in how people responded to him almost immediately. "When I made that shift, I could feel others acting differently toward me." Shortly after he energized his speaking patterns, his ESPN contract was renewed. In the year that followed, Corey estimates that about 60 percent of the games he called were on ESPN or ESPN2. He got to call a game between Virginia and Florida State, fourth- and ninth-ranked teams respectively in the country. He continued to be assigned to highly ranked games and more prestigious conferences, and by the end of the year, he'd worked five games on regular ESPN, the most he'd ever had in any sport for any season. Gaining awareness of his speaking style and slowing his pace not only effected a noticeable change to his presentation style on-air, but off-air. "In personal relationships, I say less," Corey says. "I learned to know my audience. Be efficient."

Use pace to surprise your audience, keep them engaged, and leave them wanting more. Voice coach Ellie Miller has noted that the best communicators pace their online and digital "speech," as well. "People do this with texts now. They put periods in between words for emphasis and they use capital letters and exclamation points to express themselves. This is what we should be doing with our speech."

Get into a new habit of inserting commas and adding more punctuation to your speech to separate thoughts and emphasize what you want your listener to hear. "If someone talks too rapidly or in monotones, people will listen for a minute, nod their heads, and then turn away," cautions Stephen Burdman, founder of the New York Classical Theatre. "You could have the most brilliant idea ever—you could have the cure for cancer—and no one's going to hear it if you run over or through your words."

Inflection Is Infectious

Another way to infuse energy into your voice is by adding more inflection to your words. This simple technique can turn a dull monologue into a compelling narrative that energizes your audience. I took a Shakespeare class taught by Stephen Burdman in Central Park two years ago that drove home this point. We were instructed to repeat a line of Shakespeare over and over again, and with each repetition we put emphasis on different words. So, for example, *The Merchant of Venice* opens with Antonio, the merchant of the title, saying, "In sooth, I know not why I am so sad." It's a famous line, but when you stress certain words it quickly becomes crystal clear how inflection can completely change the *meaning* of a sentence.

For example:

> In sooth, I KNOW not why I am so sad.
>
> In sooth, I know NOT why I am so sad.
>
> In sooth, I know not WHY I am so sad.
>
> In sooth, I know not why I am SO sad.
>
> In sooth, I know not why I am so SAD.

Burdman calls this "painting the picture with your words." With one adjustment to the inflection of his phrase, Antonio could be confused, conflicted, annoyed, depressed, or surprised. Depending on what word Antonio emphasizes, we get a completely different first impression of this character and his emotional state, an impression that will color our feelings about him for the rest of the play. And if the inflection isn't what we expected, we get a little jolt that makes us sit up and pay attention. The energy

Antonio emits, which will change according to his inflection, produces a similarly energized response from the audience. Keep in mind, quiet energy can be just as powerful as high energy. Low energy loses your listener; quiet energy has the power to keep people riveted in spite of themselves.

Gidi Grinstein is a well-known thought leader and the founder of the nonpartisan think tank the Reut Institute, based in Tel Aviv. Most recently he founded Tikkun Olam Makers (TOM), a global nonprofit dedicated to developing affordable solutions for the disabled, the elderly, and the poor, such as an eighty-eight-dollar wheelchair in Vietnam and other game-changing low-cost products. TOM functions by connecting "makers, inventors, and problem solvers with need-knowers—those who have a deep understanding of a real-life challenge," and getting them to work together to build a solution to that challenge. Gidi is naturally low-key, but that hasn't stopped him from successfully bringing together constituencies from often opposing viewpoints to find consensus. However, as this project required him to negotiate in bigger rooms, so to speak, that soft style wasn't working as well. He was having a hard time winning people over with the same success he'd had with other start-ups in the past. He needed to be able to inject some lightning into his otherwise consistent manner, whether he was fund-raising in a group of one to twenty or a room of hundreds. He was a quick study: "When I focused on inflection, I saw the infection on listeners in private meetings and large audiences. When you master the art of inflection, it becomes like second nature, and then you can work off the feedback you get. It becomes like a dance."

The right combination of pitch, pace, and volume will create energy in the room, and heighten it to that magic moment where you deliver the punch line. Or the bottom line. Or whatever it is you want your audience to take away and remember.

Wear Your Heart on Your Sleeve

When you're presenting to a group of people or to one person face-to-face, you have to realize that your entire body—your facial expressions, eye contact, posture, stance, and hand movements—all work together to create an impression. Bring more energy to your presentation by emotionally committing to your message. The more passionate you are about your ideas, the more physically animated you become.

Expressing higher energy with your body language does not mean you need to start gesticulating with wild abandon or punching your fist into the air to emphasize your words. Simply start paying attention to increasing the energy in your voice—matched appropriately to your surroundings, of course—and your body will naturally follow.

Take a Front Seat

Lawrence Epstein talks about being all in; I call it taking a front-row seat in life. Awhile back, I did a leadership-building seminar for an international bank. As people were filing into the conference room, I noticed the preponderance of female employees taking seats along the sides and standing in the back, intentionally choosing not to take a front-row seat. I wasn't sure if the behavior I was seeing was an issue connected to the women's titles or their gender, but either way, it didn't bode well for their professional future. While I stuck to my AWE-riginal talking points, on the spot I emphasized the importance of stepping forward and making your presence known in the room. Not everyone is born to be a leader, and it's not necessary to put yourself front and center all the time, but you can't expect to make a name for yourself if you remain invisible, either. If you're not the kind of person whose energy ensures people notice you right away, you can work on injecting your energy into the room over time. No one is going to come looking for you if you don't emit enough energy to make your presence known. When you willingly and enthusiastically inject yourself into the conversation—or even the fray—your participation generates its own energy and inspires those around you.

When Coach Tom Coughlin used to meet with his players for the first time, he would give them strict instructions on what he expected to see. "You're going to sit up in your chair. You're not going to slouch. You're going to focus your eyes on the speaker. You're not going to wear your hat in the meeting room. You're going to pay attention to detail. Have the look in your eye—the gleam. You're going to give me that kind of enthusiasm." Note that he was not demanding this behavior to get external evidence of his players' respect. He wanted them to *show* him their enthusiasm— their energy. He wanted to see their passion, how much it meant for them to be there. He was working with the same principle that says if you force yourself to smile, your brain perceives the muscle movement and releases the corresponding hormones that go with a smile, thereby actually making you feel happier. When you behave energetically, you feel more energetic. And when you feel more energetic, you genuinely exude more energy, retain what you learn, perform better, and affect people's perception of you for the better.

Commit to Service

We serve others best when we commit to excellence. I recently heard Kevin Plank, the founder of Under Armour, talk about how he came up with the idea for the product that launched a billion-dollar company, the "shorty," an athletic undershirt that wicked away moisture and stayed light and dry better than anything else out on the market. Once a college football player, he built his whole business career on performance athletic gear. And yet, he said that he would have been just as happy as a plumber, because if that's what had sparked his interest, he would have thrown himself into plumbing with the same passion he threw himself into when developing the best performance gear. He would have analyzed the materials being used and wondered what could be done to make them better. He'd be intensely focused on always being the best plumber and giving his customers the best service possible.

A devotion to excellence and service—at a professional and personal level—will always be at the hearts of any AWEsome success.

Align and Attune

You want to be energetic about how you communicate your message in a way that energizes your audience. We've all shared airspace with those who speak so frenetically and fast-paced that you feel you cannot breathe. You certainly can't get a word in and you just might suffocate from being overwhelmed before they finish their string of run-on sentences. You've probably also experienced the dinner guest who speaks in long mono-logues without inviting anyone else to contribute, and *then* who concludes at the end of the meal, "What a great conversation." *Say what?* That wasn't a conversation. You spoke the entire time! If you're solely focused on the output of your message and un-receptive to input, you won't energize your audience. In fact, you can easily deflate them because they will *feel* if you're only focused on yourself.

Rebecca Stuard is the co-head of Improvolution, which trains businesspeople in the craft of improv. Stuard teaches her students to "listen with your whole body—you don't just listen with your ears. You listen with your eyes. You listen with your movements, all of it." When your audience feels acknowledged and that their input is received, they feel engaged, which in itself is energizing. From there, if you then invite your audience into the conversation, they become even more animated. I enjoy Broadway shows when the actors, singers, and dancers come out into the audience and get people on their feet. One can't help but feel a heightened energy in the air. We can each replicate a version of this by engaging our audience and creating an energy flow back and forth.

"When you listen to someone you're, in effect, listening to their rhythm," says Stuard. "And there is a flow that happens when you get on what I call *their rhythm train*. Communication becomes so much easier when you're aware of another person's rhythm because you can then get into rhythm *with* them." Gidi Grinstein says some of his favorite moments with his friend the *New York Times* columnist Tom Friedman is when they're "jamming" together. They're exchanging ideas, not playing music, but the effect is the same as they feed off each other's energy. The rhythm train, jamming, or whatever you call it, that feeling you get when you're in alignment and attunement with another person and building toward the same goal is simply another version of what psychologist Mihaly Csikszentmihalyi labeled "flow."

We've talked a lot about deep listening, how it brings people in, builds trust, and makes people feel acknowledged. It's also key to growing energy. Again, you're making room for input. Think about how you've felt when you've wanted to talk to someone about something that matters to you, or that you're excited about, and you realize they're not paying attention, or even only half paying attention. Think about how it feels to be dismissed or ignored. It's awful. It's dispiriting and discouraging, and sometimes even humiliating. It saps your energy. It's impossible to build consensus, community, or common cause when you don't listen deeply and respond in a way that proves you heard, you care, and you understand (politicians, take note).

One excellent way to make sure people feel heard and energized is to improve your memory. Mad Dog Russo says his excellent memory is one of the attributes that make him such a popular sports radio talk-show host. "If you can remember certain games historically, that can go a long way. Because very few people can do that. Many of the people who call in are older men, and they want to break down the 1967 Packers. I can do that." Mad Dog was eight years old in 1967, but he can tell you all the details of that football season, as well as pretty much any other. He uses his memory to connect better with his callers. You can do the exact same thing in your daily life. It's easy when you make it a point to listen well. When you meet and engage with people, it shouldn't feel transactional. Think of each encounter as an opportunity to learn something new about another person, to hear about what matters to them or what's on their radar.

Let's say you attend a business function and meet Dave, who is gearing up for his daughter's bat mitzvah. Six months later, you're at another event and you bump into Dave again, only this time you're in the company of casual business acquaintance Jolene, whose oldest daughter is about to get married. You can build a lot of energy and goodwill with Dave if you remember to ask him about the bat mitzvah and appear genuinely interested to hear the details. You'll build even more energy when you draw Jolene into the conversation by pointing out that she, too, is about to watch her child step through a major rite of passage.

You've made both feel acknowledged, proving that when you talk to them, you're actually paying attention and care enough to retain what they tell you, even if it's not relevant to you or to whatever business you're conducting together. You've connected and engaged with Dave, with Jolene, and best of all, you've sparked a new connection between the two of them.

Or say you have a new employee, Joel, who somewhere along the way mentioned that he was an only child. One day you invite the team out to lunch, and another employee, Siobhan, mentions that one of her sisters just gave birth to twins, which now means she has nine nieces and nephews, and you say, "Congratulations! Man, that must have been crazy, growing up with seven brothers and sisters. Dave here is an only child. You probably can't even imagine that, right, Siobhan?" Boom. Connection made. Most likely, Siobhan and Dave, and maybe even everyone at the table, are going to start sharing stories about growing up in their respective families, highlighting the differences and, who knows, maybe even the similarities. You've created a connection, but you've also subtly let Dave know that when he talks about himself, you're listening, and you care enough to remember. You've built trust. When you let the world know that people are important to you all the time, not just when they have something you need, you will go a long way toward building a strong, vibrant community around yourself.

Make it a point to become a catalyst between people, not because it gets you anything down the line, but because the world needs us to create more sparks of light.

CONCLUSION | GROW OR DIE

In the twenty-five years I've been a talent agent and performance coach, I've learned that there are two types of ambitious people: diligent, committed individuals who develop strong reputations for their expertise and effectiveness, and diligent, committed individuals who develop strong reputations for their expertise and effectiveness and *also* achieve the highest levels of professional and personal success. What makes the difference?

One takes yes for an answer; the other doesn't.

The greatest musicians, athletes, or performers in the world don't care how good they are; they care about getting even better. They are their own most effective critics. Universally, those who reach the pinnacles of their career and are lauded as the best in their fields are relentless in their pursuit of excellence. They're never satisfied, no matter how many "yesses" life—or well-meaning peers, family members, co-workers, or bosses–offers them. Notably, the people they respect the most are usually not the ones who tell them they're doing great, but the ones brave enough to tell them where they can do more.

You might worry that asking for honest, constructive feedback might expose you to constant, painful amounts of criticism and negativity, and indeed that would be terrible if it happened. But it won't, not if you change your mind-set about what it is you seek. You're not looking for criticism; you're looking for ways to get better. When you take that perspective, and you know the person giving you the feedback you've asked for has your best interest at heart and is coming from a constructive place, it doesn't hurt. Nothing ever feels like a put-down. It all just becomes more fuel to get you where you want to be. And once you see how much addressing that critique benefits you professionally, you'll be eager to apply this mind-set to the rest of your life.

One way to create that mind-set is to follow the sage advice of Chuck D. from Public Enemy, who said simply, "Don't Believe the Hype." You can find courage in proactive humility (think of it as a "yes" filter). I teach this stuff and I still have to work on it myself. For example, in the run-up to writing this book, I started doing a bunch of speaking engagements and made guest appearances on a number of podcasts. Each time I'd walk off the stage or leave the studio, I'd hear a chorus of "good jobs." Of course that made me feel great. Then I asked a few friends to really listen to the podcast and give me their feedback. One in particular is a seasoned trial lawyer and knows how to win a room. I trusted him. So when he came back with a pat on the back, I challenged him as a favor to listen again and point out two things upon which I could improve. We got together for dinner a few days later. He spent the first fifteen minutes giving me feedback on the two things I asked him to pay attention to, and then the next thirty minutes on four other things I didn't even think I needed to work on! And he was right about every single point. I conducted the same exercise with my brother—also an attorney—regarding a different but also extensively praised podcast and received almost the same litany of constructive comments. The truth was, I really wasn't that good! Hopefully by the time this book is published and I start making the podcast rounds again, I'll be as good as I aspire to be. Who knows, maybe that's how you found this book in the first place.

It's easy to demand critique and feedback when you ascribe to the philosophy of "grow or die." What's harder is convincing people that you mean it. For all the reasons we explained in the early chapters of this book, most people will hesitate to tell you what they really think. So it's up to you to make it safe for others to be constructively tough on you. You may have to explicitly demand it. Make sure people understand that you don't want anything to come between you and your goals. If you're a manager who wants your team to be honest with you, it's up to you to build a culture that encourages trust and communication. My employees know they should never be afraid to tell me what they think, and I go out of my way to praise and thank them when they offer me a direct critique. I've spent years proving to them over and over that there are no repercussions for speaking their mind. You can start that process now.

Begin by prefacing every interaction with clients, employers, or peers with an invitation to tell you how you could improve whatever it is you're doing with or for them at that moment. Thank them when they comply, and the next time you see them, make sure they can see the work you've put in to get better. Then ask, was that more effective? More efficient? More reassuring? More direct? If they say no, try again the next chance you get, and ask them again for their thoughts. Yes? Keep it up, and ask them again for their thoughts. As you can see, the process never ends. Obviously you will have to get really good at reading the room. If you can tell you're making someone uncomfortable by pressing them for feedback, turn to someone else another time. But if you're using AWE, you'll find that many people will be willing to give you the information you need.

When we're just starting out, Energy is practically all we've got to offer the world. As we gain experience and expertise, we can start working on establishing our Authority. Warmth is directly connected to our levels of confidence, which means the older and wiser we get, the warmer we should get, too. I hope this book has provided many "aha" moments as you begin to understand how your "performance"—how you present yourself in public and private—is either helping or hurting you. How you speak, hold, and carry yourself; your overall vibe; your habits, behaviors, actions, and reactions all create an *impression* and the question is: What is that impression that you're making, moment to moment? If you're finding yourself lacking by a little or a lot, don't fret. That's the beauty of AWE—*it's never too early or too late to get more.*

Let's say that before you began this program, you had a habit of looking down or away when you spoke to people, giving the impression that you lacked confidence in your message and ideas. This habit had been undermining your authority, and also your warmth, but you weren't aware of it. I call this *unconscious incompetency.* Through observation of those around you, followed by self-inquiry and assessment, you gained AWE-wareness that you didn't have before. At this point, you entered the next stage—*conscious incompetency.* You became aware of how a lack of authority was impeding your ability to make positive impressions on people and, in some way, stalling your success.

Now, by working on correcting specific behaviors and creating new habits that encourage more connection, you're in a conscious stage of change. Once I became aware of my habit of crossing my arms at parties, giving the impression that I was defensive or closed off, I consciously made the effort to change. As I created a new habit of uncrossing my arms I become *consciously competent.* With practice and repetition, now without even thinking about it, I comfortably leave my arms at my side. My hope for you is that eventually your new habit of listening and looking directly at people when they speak, for example, will become so natural and automatic that it becomes unconscious. It's just what you do on instinct. Like a great serve at Wimbledon. Or playing music by ear. When you're correcting your negative behaviors as if on autopilot, you've entered the stage of *unconscious competency*, which signifies a new personal standard. A new level of AWEsome.

Keep your standards high, work hard, and go get that dream job—this book is definitely not against that kind of effort. Gone are the days when we could coast on a fancy academic degree or job titles. They can open doors, but it's AWE that will propel you through them. If you're hardworking and ambitious enough to achieve your goal, you're smart and savvy enough to realize it's just a starting point. We are always capable of more than we think we are. AWE just helps us prove it to everyone else, too.

On May 6, 1954, Roger Bannister became the first athlete to break the four-minute mile when he ran 3:59.4. Considered an unbreakable barrier, Bannister became world famous for reaching "one of man's hitherto unattainable goals." But then, over the next decade, his groundbreaking record was reduced to 3:54.1; then again to 3:50 in 1975, and in 1999 Hicham El Guerrouj set the current world record of 3:43.13. Once Bannister rose what was considered an impossible bar, others surpassed it. And when the mile no longer remained the standard, improvement stopped dead in its tracks.

The meaning for you: Even *after* you've achieved a level of unconscious competency, continue to reset your standards and you will meet them. Raise your bar even higher, and you're likely to reach it.

"The people who make it look easy and natural have worked their butts off," says Professor Barry Friedman.

He's right. Improvement is work. Don't let that stop you. It makes the difference between mediocrity and true achievement. With practice and heightened AWE-wareness you will become your own master.

And it doesn't get more AWEsome than that.

No matter what we build, we never do it completely alone. Behind us is always someone who lent an encouraging word, opened a door (or at least pointed it out), made a fortuitous introduction, or provided their skills and expertise. The same is true here.

This book was conceived from a simple question during a speech Talee Potter hired me to give at Bank Leumi in 2016: "Where can I buy a copy of your book for my children?" That lead to a conversation that night with my wife, Raquel, who matter-of-factly said, "Start writing it NOW." Luckily, I listen to my wife, and thirty pages came spilling out of me. A chance encounter with Jill Zucker led me to Yfat Reiss Gendell at the Foundry Literary Agency, who skillfully introduced me to the shepherds of this book, Stephanie Hitchcock and Hollis Heimbouch at HarperCollins. Many thanks to all for your early support and enthusiasm for this project.

Along the way, I had the chance to work with two gifted writers: Samantha Rose, who was instrumental in the process—and Stephanie Land, who, for lack of a better word, was AWEsome.

So many people were incredibly generous with their time and feedback; it would require a dozen pages to properly thank them. My partner Sandy Montag went above and beyond to help secure many of the people interviewed on these pages and I am grateful for both his help and the friendship we have cultivated over almost three decades, and the partnership that is nearly four years old now.

Over the past near quarter century of running a business, I've had the chance to work with some talented people, many of whom have transcended business and become close friends. Three of my first clients, dating back to the last century—Dave Revsine, Brian Anderson, and Dan Shulman—all lent their wisdom and time. Greg Amsinger and Liam McHugh were equally generous. I'd also like to thank many others who agreed to sit down and talk to me (some on background) including Ari Fleischer, Tom Coughlin, Stephanie Druley, Al Jaffe, Kenny Plotnik, Admiral Mike Mullen, Joe Torre, Dan Senor, Alyssa Mastromonaco, Barry Friedman, Lawrence Epstein, Dari Nowkhah, Mike Corey, Christopher Russo, Ken Langone, Stephen Burdman, Sean McManus, Josie Thomas, Rebecca Stuard, Zachary Farden, Ellie Miller, Ed Tiryakian, Mike Novogratz, Joel Segal, Charlie Linville, Steven Shapiro, Dr. Alec Miller, Peter Bregman, Michael Borkow, Dr. Michael Levine, Dr. Robert Goldstein, Paul Finebaum, Holly Rowe, Ritcha Ranjan, Mitch Rubin, Catherine Rampell, Dr. John Torres, Lauren Glassberg, Sam Flood, Clarissa Ward, Laura Slabin, Andrew Slabin, Scott Moore, Suzy Kolber, Beth Mowins, Scott Metcalfe, Dick Vitale, Tiki Barber, Elena Shemetoff, Tammy Stern, Connor Schell, Doug Gottlieb, Harvey Potter, Reid Pakula, Gidi Grinstein, Moshe Horn, Jeff Feig, Christopher Akpobiyeri, and Steven Cohen.

I'd also like to thank my colleagues at the Montag Group and IF Management. Gideon Cohen and Carol Perry have been a part of my life for over two decades as co-workers and have become like family. Michael Sones and Kevin Belbey helped with the program on which this book was written. Jeff Feldman has been my invaluable communication sparring partner since the day he graduated college and joined our company almost fifteen years ago. My partner Maury Gostfrand was gracious and helpful in setting up a key interview and encouraging me every step of the way.

Only a few people read the materials during the writing process and they had excellent comments. I particularly appreciate Natalya Emanuel; Alec Sirken; my wife, Raquel; and my brother, Arnie Herz, for their time and valuable comments.

Finally, thanks to my family for their support. My children, Josie and Jack, who have embraced the concepts in this book even in their preteen years. My parents, Myra and Stu Herz, have always been unwavering in their belief in me.

And if I have unintentionally forgotten anyone who lent their support, please accept my apologies and my deepest appreciation.

Chapter 1: What's Blocking You?

15   a seminal study: "The Soft Skills Disconnect," National Soft Skills Association, February 23, 2015, http://www.nationalsoftskills.org /the-soft-skills-disconnect/.

15   the findings of this study: "The Real Skills Gap," National Soft Skills Association, April 8, 2016, http://www.nationalsoftskills.org /the-real-skills-gap/.

16   extrapolating the data: "The Soft Skills Disconnect," National Soft Skills Association, February 23, 2015, https://www.nationalsoftskills.org /the-soft-skills-disconnect/.

16   nontechnical social skills: "Bridging the Soft Skills Gap," U.S. Chamber of Commerce Foundation, Allegheny Conference on Community Development, 2015, 6, http://simplysuccess.com/wp-content/uploads/2016/08 /BridgingSoftSkillsGap_US_Chamber_of_Commerce_Foundation.pdf.

16   In a *Wall Street Journal* survey: Kate Davidson, "Employers Find 'Soft Skills' Like Critical Thinking in Short Supply," *Wall Street Journal*, August 30, 2016, http://www.wsj.com/articles/employers-find-soft-skills-like-critical-thinking-in-short-supply-1472549400?emailToken=e394ceb45d4490d080 71d4980d39aa9b%2FrXlH8wb5Zdc2i4I1ZtNyipQdso3KzDiZpGQY 9cYmaLCeaUqxGhDJCNQMRh4OTCti4ZIAskxUZZ7Zm8VGolLlhaMy 5CVdAWLQI70lAKWerwPlcwJzFGOFHN%2Ba0t6u0Cu.

16   a LinkedIn survey: Guy Berger, "Data Reveals the Most In-Demand Soft Skills Among Candidates," *LinkedIn Talent Blog*, August 30, 2016, https:// business.linkedin.com/talent-solutions/blog/trends-and-research/2016 /most-indemand-soft-skills.

16   One Harvard paper: Andy Rosen, "The Golden Ticket to Higher Paying Jobs: Hard Skills Plus Social Skills," *Boston Globe*, November 16, 2017, https://www.bostonglobe.com/business/specials/top-places-to -work/2017/11/16/the-golden-ticket-higher-paying-jobs-hard-skills-plus -social-skills/FosGMoHKlOZ3fEWEHvevkN/story.html.

16   Even in technical careers: "The Soft Skills Stats You Need to Know," *Coursera Blog*, August 16, 2017, https://blog.coursera.org/soft-skills-stats-need-know/.

16   Google's Project Oxygen: Cathy N. Davidson, "The Surprising Thing Google Learned about Its Employees—and What It Means for Today's Students," *Washington Post*, December 20, 2017, http://www.nationalsoftskills.org/not-surprising-thing-google-learned-employees/.

16   Silicon Valley companies: Claire Cain Miller, "Tech's Damaging Myth of the Loner Genius Nerd," *New York Times*, August 12, 2017, https://www.nytimes.com/2017/08/12/upshot/techs-damaging-myth-of-the-loner-genius-nerd.html.

17   63 percent: "Bridging the Soft Skills Gap," U.S. Chamber of Commerce Foundation, Allegheny Conference on Community Development, 2015, 9, http://simplysuccess.com/wp-content/uploads/2016/08/BridgingSoftSkillsGap_US_Chamber_of_Commerce_Foundation.pdf.

17   many companies are investing: Davidson, "Employers Find 'Soft Skills' Like Critical Thinking in Short Supply."

18   research shows: Amy Ashmore, "Seven Seconds to Success," *PsychCentral* (blog), last updated July 8, 2018, https://psychcentral.com/blog/seven-seconds-to-success/.

18   our initial impression: J. Willis and A. Todorov, "First Impressions: Making Up Your Mind After a 100-ms Exposure to a Face," *Psychology Science*, July 17, 2006, https://www.ncbi.nlm.nih.gov/pubmed/16866745.

18   Those very first impressions: Rosie Ifould, "Acting on Impulse," *Guardian*, March 6, 2009, https://www.theguardian.com/lifeandstyle/2009/mar/07/first-impressions-snap-decisions-impulse.

24   That rule has been widely misinterpreted: Albert Mehrabian, "'Silent Messages'—A Wealth of Information about Nonverbal Communication (Body Language)," accessed August 26, 2019, http://www.kaaj.com/psych/smorder.html.

25   "Henry Higgins": Margalit Fox, "Sam Chwat, Dialect Tutor for Film Stars, Dies at 57," *New York Times*, March 8, 2011, https://www.nytimes.com/2011/03/08/nyregion/08chwat.html.

26   "shit": Erika Adams, "Ralph Lauren's American Dream," Racked, July 26, 2016, https://www.racked.com/2016/7/26/12274000/ralph-lauren.

26   not because he wanted to erase: "Oprah Talks to Ralph Lauren," O, *The Oprah Magazine*, October 2002, http://www.oprah.com/omagazine/oprah-interviews-ralph-lauren/10.

27 By some estimates: Lou Adler, "New Survey Reveals 85% of All Jobs are Filled Via Networking," LinkedIn, February 29, 2016, https://www.linkedin .com/pulse/new-survey-reveals-85-all-jobs-filled-via-networking-lou-adler/.

27 "'who you know' often mirrors": Jennifer Merluzzi and Adina Sterling, "Research: Black Employees Are More Likely to Be Promoted When They Were Referred by Another Employee," *Harvard Business Review*, February 28, 2017, https://hbr.org/2017/02/research-black-employees-are-more-likely-to-be-promoted-when-they-were-referred-by-another-employee.

Chapter 2: The Problem with Yes

33 "party favors": Betty Berdan, "Participation Trophies Send a Dangerous Message," *New York Times*, October 6, 2016, https://www.nytimes.com /roomfordebate/2016/10/06/should-every-young-athlete-get-a-trophy /participation-trophies-send-a-dangerous-message.

34 the incentives for elite: Jenny Anderson, "Rich Kids' Grades Are Rising Faster, and Intelligence Probably Isn't the Reason Why," *Quartz*, August 21, 2017, https://qz.com/1058476/grade-inflation-is-the-worst-at-rich-private -schools-disadvantaging-poor-students/.

34 most significantly: Ibid.

34 that's about one in four: Sarah Butrymowicz, "Most Colleges Enroll Students Who Aren't Prepared for Higher Education," *PBS NewsHour*, January 30, 2017, https://www.pbs.org/newshour/education /colleges-enroll-students-arent-prepared-higher-education.

35 According to a study: Scott Jaschik, "Grade Inflation, Higher and Higher," Inside Higher Ed, March 29, 2016, https://www.insidehighered. com/news/2016/03/29/survey-finds-grade-inflation-continues -rise-four-year-colleges-not-community-college.

36 Career coach Dan Miller: Dan Miller, "Nobody Gets 'Fired' Anymore," 48 Days, https://www.48days.com/nobody-gets-fired-anymore/.

36 which is most of them: Andrew Soergel, "Most of America's Businesses Run by White Men," *U.S. News*, September 1, 2016, https://www.usnews.com/news/articles/2016-09-01 /most-of-americas-businesses-run-by-white-men-says-census-bureau.

36 women, and men and women of color: Sylvia Ann Hewlett, *Executive Presence: The Missing Link Between Merit and Success* (New York: Harper Business, 2014), 109–10.

36 any assessment specifically on appearance: Ibid., 110–11.

37   many HR professionals: Liz Ryan, "Five Things the HR Department Won't Tell You," *Forbes*, January 9, 2017, https://www.forbes.com/sites/lizryan/2017/01/09/five-things-the-hr-department-wont-tell-you/2/#2da467ed3845.

37   The formal performance improvement plan: J. T. O'Donnell, "10 Things HR Doesn't Want You to Know (But I'll Tell You)," *Inc.*, October 6, 2015, https://www.inc.com/jt-odonnell/10-things-hr-doesn-t-want-you-to-know-but-i-ll-tell-you.html.

37   many employers: Susan M. Heathfield, "10 Things You Should Never Do When Firing an Employee," TheBalanceCareers.com, updated June 25, 2019, https://www.thebalance.com/top-10-don-ts-when-you-fire-an-employee-1918343.

39   one of the most famous lines: "Your Altitude," Ziglar, https://www.ziglar.com/quotes/your-attitude-not-your-aptitude/.

40   "the counterfeit yes": Christopher Voss, *Never Split the Difference* (New York: Harper Business, 2016), 80–81.

Chapter 4: Command Authority

47   immensely popular class: Eleanor Dearman, "Texas State Capitol Hosts Exhibit Honoring Civil Rights Activist Barbara Jordan," *The Daily Texan*, February 11, 2015, https://www.dailytexanonline.com/2015/02/11/texas-state-capitol-hosts-exhibit-honoring-civil-rights-activist-barbara-jordan.

50   Mort Cooper wrote: Morton Cooper, *Change Your Voice, Change Your Life: A Quick and Simple Plan for Finding & Using Your Natural Dynamic Voice* (New York: Macmillan, 1984), 34.

53   Some suggest that we associate: Katrina Onstad, "Up High or Down Low: What a Woman's Voice Says about Her," *The Globe and Mail*, updated May 9, 2018, https://www.theglobeandmail.com/life/relationships/up-high-or-down-low-what-a-womans-voice-says-about-her/article1359268/.

53   Another theory is: Megan Garber, "Why We Prefer Masculine Voices (Even in Women)," *Atlantic*, December 18, 2012, https://www.theatlantic.com/sexes/archive/2012/12/why-we-prefer-masculine-voices-even-in-women/266350/.

53   In a Duke University study: William J. Mayhew et al., "Voice Pitch and the Labor Market Success of Male Chief Executive Officers," *Evolution and Human Behavior* 34, no. 4 (July 2013): 243–48, https://www.sciencedirect.com/science/article/pii/S1090513813000238?_ga=2.142749813.175933119.1559868589-1532255238.1559868589.

59   He was concerned: Kenneth Feinberg, interview with Alex Blumberg, "The Tragedy Expert," April 8, 2019, in *Without Fail*, podcast audio, https:// gimletmedia.com/shows/without-fail/5who4m.

60   Legendary basketball coach: Dennis Hevesi, "Frank Mickens, Who Brought Success to a Tough Brooklyn High School, Dies at 63," *New York Times*, July 10, 2009, https://www.nytimes.com/2009/07/11/nyregion/11mickens.html.

61   one of the most: Sean Leslie, "Which Three States Have the Most Formal Office Dress Codes?" Payscale.com, February 9, 2017, https://www.payscale .com/career-news/2017/02/states-with-most-formal-office-dress-codes.

61   They believe that: Leonard L. Berry and Neelie Bendapudi, "Clueing in Customers—Why Docs Don't Wear White Coats or Polo Shirts at the Mayo Clinic," HBS.edu, March 17, 2003, https://hbswk.hbs.edu/archive /clueing-in-customers-why-docs-don-t-wear-white-coats-or-polo-shirts-at -the-mayo-clinic.

61   When administrator: Ibid.

67   "biggest badass": Brian Flood, "Why CNN's Clarissa Ward May Be the Biggest Badass in Cable News," TheWrap.com, April 10, 2016, https:// www.thewrap.com/why-cnns-clarissa-ward-may-be-the-biggest-badass-in -cable-news/.

Chapter 6: Warmth: The Seed of Trust

88   "'You know what'": Lori Gottlieb, *Maybe You Should Talk to Someone: A Therapist, Her Therapist, and Our Lives Revealed* (New York: Houghton Mifflin Harcourt, 2019), 114.

88   For example, a 2017 study: Timothy J. Cunningham et al., "Vital Signs: Racial Disparities in Age-Specific Mortality Among Blacks or African Americans—United States, 1999–2015," *Morbidity and Mortality Weekly Report* 66, no. 17 (May 2017): 444–456, https://www.cdc.gov/mmwr /volumes/66/wr/mm6617e1.htm.

88   after which: Gina Kolata, "Black Americans Are Living Longer, C.D.C. Re-ports," *New York Times*, May 2, 2017, https://www.nytimes .com/2017/05/02/health/black-americans-death-rate-cdc-study.html.

89   Closing that gap: Cunningham et al., "Vital Signs."

89   a rate that saw: Jay Fitzgerald, "Tuskegee, Trust in Doctors, and the Health of Black Men," *NBER Digest*, August 2016, 2–3, https://www.nber.org /digest/aug16/aug16.pdf.

89   In 2018, researchers: Nicole Torres, "Research: Having a Black Doctor Led

Black Men to Receive More Effective Care," *Harvard Business Review*, August 10, 2018, https://hbr.org/2018/08/research-having-a-black-doctor-led-black-men-to-receive-more-effective-care.

90   According to Owen Garrick: "Researchers May Have Found a Way to Improve Black Men's Life Expectancy," NPR.org, June 13, 2019, https://www.npr.org/2019/06/13/732270787/researchers-may-have-found-a-way-to-improve-the-life-expectancy-of-black-men.

90   There are other: Torres, "Research."

92   when they feel pressured: Herminia Ibarra, "The Authenticity Paradox," HBR.org, January/February 2015, https://hbr.org/2015/01/the-authenticity-paradox.

92   people suspect: Melody Wilding, "Being Vulnerable at Work Can Backfire," Quartz.com, December 14, 2017, https://qz.com/work/1155447/being-vulnerable-at-work-can-backfire/.

92   "You don't stand": Kimberly Weisul, "Why the Best Leaders Are Vulnerable," Inc.com, June 11, 2013, https://www.inc.com/kimberly-weisul/leadership-why-the-best-leaders-are-vulnerable.html.

92   vulnerability and courage: Gregory Lewis, "Why Being Vulnerable at Work Can Be Your Biggest Advantage, According to Brené Brown," LinkedIn.com, October 4, 2017, https://business.linkedin.com/talent-solutions/blog/talent-connect/2017/why-being-vulnerable-at-work-can-be-your-biggest-advantage-according-to-brene-brown.

92   "Vulnerability is the birthplace": Helen Walters, "Vulnerability is the birthplace of innovation, creativity, and change: Brené Brown at TED2012," *TED blog*, March 2, 2012, https://blog.ted.com/vulnerability-is-the-birthplace-of-innovation-creativity-and-change-brene-brown-at-ted2012/.

93   dress socks only: Michelle Kapusta, "This NFL Coach Runs a 'Dictatorship,' According to 1 Player," Sportscasting.com, April 8, 2018, https://www.sportscasting.com/nfl/nfl-coach-runs-dictatorship-according-one-player/.

93   white socks only: Bill Pennington, "Coughlin Goes by the Book, and Wins," *New York Times*, January 21, 2012, https://www.nytimes.com/2012/01/22/sports/football/tom-coughlin-goes-by-the-book-and-wins.html.

93   One anonymous: Kapusta, "This NFL Coach Runs a 'Dicatorship.'"

93   Hall of Fame defensive end: Nick Schwartz, "Cowherd: Michael Strahan Opens Up on How the Giants Used to Hate Tom Coughlin," FoxSports.com, February 2, 2017, https://www.foxsports.com/nfl/story/cowherd

-michael-strahan-opens-up-on-how-the-giants-used-to-hate-tom-coughlin
-020217.

94   Another anonymous teammate: "Let the Record Show: Players 'Hate'
      Coughlin," 247sports.com, December 26, 2004, https://247sports.com
      /nfl/new-york-giants/Article/Let-the-record-show-Players-hate-Coughlin
      -104158327/.

94   "free fallen": John Branch, "Coughlin Demotes Offensive Coordinator,"
      New York Times, December 27, 2006, https://www.nytimes.com
      /2006/12/27/sports/football/27giants.html.

94   "spent more time": Ian O'Connor, "How Tom Coughlin Changed His Ways
      and Won Over the Giants," ESPN.com, January 5, 2016, https://
      www.espn.com/nfl/story/_/id/14504114/how-tom-coughlin-changed
      -ways-won-new-york-giants-nfl.

94   During the second half: John Branch, "Coughlin Demotes Offensive Co-
      ordinator," *New York Times*, December 27, 2006, https://www.nytimes.
      com/2006/12/27/sports/football/27giants.html.

94   After mulling over: Ian O'Connor, "How Tom Coughlin Changed His Ways
      and Won Over the Giants," ESPN, January 5, 2016, http://www.espn.com
      /nfl/story/_/id/14504114/how-tom-coughlin-changed-ways-won-new-york
      -giants-nfl.

95   "It was fun": O'Connor, "How Tom Coughlin Changed His Ways and Won
      Over the Giants."

98   "Holly's energy": Holly Rowe, "Holly Rowe: 20 Years With ESPN and More
      to Come," ESPNFrontRow.com, May 18, 2017, https://www.espnfrontrow
      .com/2017/05/holly-rowe-20-years-espn-come/.

100   Arms tightly folded: Leonard Mlodinow, "How We Communicate Through
      Body Language," PsychologyToday.com, May 29, 2012, https://
      www.psychologytoday.com/us/blog/subliminal/201205/how-we
      -communicate-through-body-language.

104   Acknowledgment is crucial: "For Better Customer Service, Offer Options,
      Not Apologies," in *HBR IdeaCast*, podcast audio, 27:00, https://itunes
      .apple.com/us/podcast/hbr-ideacast/id152022135?mt=2&i=1000400009433.

106   By paying almost double: Aine Cain, "Costco Employees Share the 7
      Best Parts of Working at the Retail Chain with a Cult-like Following," Busi-
      nessInsider.com, April 3, 2018, https://www.businessinsider.com
      /costco-jobs-best-part-2018-4#the-majority-of-workers-said
      -that-pay-benefits-and-job-security-are-a-huge-draw-1.

107   His approach drew criticism: Steven Greenhouse, "How Costco Became
       the Anti-Wal-Mart," *New York Times*, July 17, 2005, https://www.nytimes
       .com/2005/07/17/business/yourmoney/how-costco-became-the-anti
       -walmart.html.

107   Sinegal insisted: Melissa Campanelli, "A Few Thoughts from Costco's Jim
       Sinegal," MyTotalRetail.com, November 1, 2017, https://www.mytotal
       retail.com/post/a-few-thoughts-from-costcos-jim-sinegal/.

107   With a 12.9 percent annual growth: Tom Relihan, "How Costco's
       Obsession with Culture Drove Success," MITSloan, May 11, 2018,
       https://mitsloan.mit.edu/ideas-made-to-matter/how-costcos
       -obsession-culture-drove-success.

107   rates of employee theft: Andrew Bary, "One Secret to Costco's Success:
       A Tight Rein on Shoplifting," Barrons.com, last updated May 30, 2019,
       https://www.barrons.com/articles/costco-earnings-shoplifting
       -51559067930.

Chapter 7: Turn Up Your Warmth

116   "Don't fake it": Amy Cuddy, "Your Body Language Shapes Who You Are,"
       TedGlobal 2012, https://www.ted.com/talks/amy_cuddy_your_body
       _language_shapes_who_you_are?language=en.

Chapter 8: Energy Draws the World In

127   cultivated a reputation: David L. Judson Jr., "On the Inside Track," *Vander-
       bilt Lawyer* 40, no. 1, https://law.vanderbilt.edu/alumni/lawyer
       -vol40num1/inside_track-epstein.html.

128   It was banned: Rory Aldo, "History of Mixed Martial Arts," MMAODDS
       .com, 2015, https://www.mmaodds.com/history-of-mma/.

128   one of the sumo: "UFC 1 Starts with 'Kick Heard 'Round the World,'"
       BoxingInsider.com, February 15, 2011, https://www.boxinginsider.com/
       mma/ufc-1-starts-with-%E2%80%9Ckick-heard-%E2%80%99round-the-
       world%E2%80%9D/.

129   in 2016: "New York Legalizes MMA After Nearly 20-Year Ban on the
       Sport," FoxSports.com, March 22, 2016, https://www.foxsports.com
       /ufc/story/ufc-new-york-legalizes-mma-after-nearly-20-year-ban-on-the
       -sport-032216.

129   broke every UFC record: Damon Martin, "Here Are All the Records UFC
       205: Alvarez vs. McGregor shattered on Saturday," UFC.com, December 9,

2016, https://www.foxsports.com/ufc/story/here-are-all-the-records-ufc -205-alvarez-vs-mcgregor-shattered-on-saturday-111516.

134 "character excavations": David Segal, "Confessor. Feminist. Adult. What the Hell Happened to Howard Stern?" *New York Times*, July 27, 2016, https:// www.nytimes.com/2016/07/31/arts/howard-stern-sirius.html?_r=0.

135 "his interest in people": Ibid.

138 Professor Frank Bernieri: Rosie Ifould, "Acting on Impulse," *Guardian*, March 7, 2009, https://www.theguardian.com/lifeandstyle/2009/mar/07 /first-impressions-snap-decisions-impulse.

Chapter 9: Turn Up Your Energy

152 Mike Corey: ESPN Press Room, "Play by Play," ESPNpressroom.com, https://espnpressroom.com/us/bios/mike-corey/.

156 "need-knowers": TOM: Tikkun Olam Makers, "TOM: Makers for People with Disabilities—How It Works," YouTube video, https://www.youtube .com/watch?v=gKJQ2B0QW1s.

158 the same principle: Nicole Spector, "Smiling Can Trick Your Brain into Happiness—and Boost Your Health," NBCnews.com, November 28, 2017, https://www.nbcnews.com/better/health/smiling-can-trick -your-brain-happiness-boost-your-health-ncna822591.

Conclusion: Grow or Die

167 On May 6, 1954: Frank Litsky and Bruce Weber, "Roger Bannister, First Athlete to Break the 4-Minute Mile, Dies at 88," *New York Times*, March 24, 2018, https://www.nytimes.com/2018/03/04/obituaries /roger-bannister-dead.html.

As the president and founding partner of IF Management and now president of the Montag Group, *STEVE HERZ* is an influential voice in broadcasting and a respected business leader. He lives in New York City with his wife and two kids.